CANADIAN CHALLENGES

Don Quinlan
Series Editor

World Affairs Defining Canada's Role

Ian Henderson   Peter Lawley   Norm Probert   Don Quinlan

CONTENTS

All terms appearing in boldfaced type in the text are defined in the Glossary that appears on page 96.

FOCUS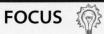

This section will help you understand
a. Canada's role in world affairs at the turn of the century.

> **The twentieth century will belong to Canada.**
> —Sir Wilfrid Laurier,
> Prime Minister of Canada from 1896 to 1911.

Figure 1-1 Wilfrid Laurier.

The Canadian Challenge

In 1900 Canada seemed like a wonderful place to live. It was peaceful for one thing, with plenty of room and hundreds of acres of rich land free for the asking. In this sense, it had little in common with Europe's dark, overcrowded cities. For a young person with energy and vision, Prime Minister Laurier's claim that the 20th century would belong to Canada probably seemed prophetic.

Millions of people in Europe thought so. They packed up their belongings and left everything they knew behind to try their luck in Canada. In 1901, fully 13% of the Canadian population consisted of recent immigrants. Immigration reached a peak in 1913, when Canada welcomed 400 000 new residents, a figure that has never come close to being equalled since.

The Canadian economy was booming and cities were expanding rapidly. By 1910 Montreal had 500 000 residents, Toronto 400 000, and Vancouver 100 000. But the waves of immigrants did not settle only in the cities. There were so many settlers eager to farm in Canada's prairie lands that in 1905 two new provinces were created—Saskatchewan and Alberta.

TIMELINE 1900-2000

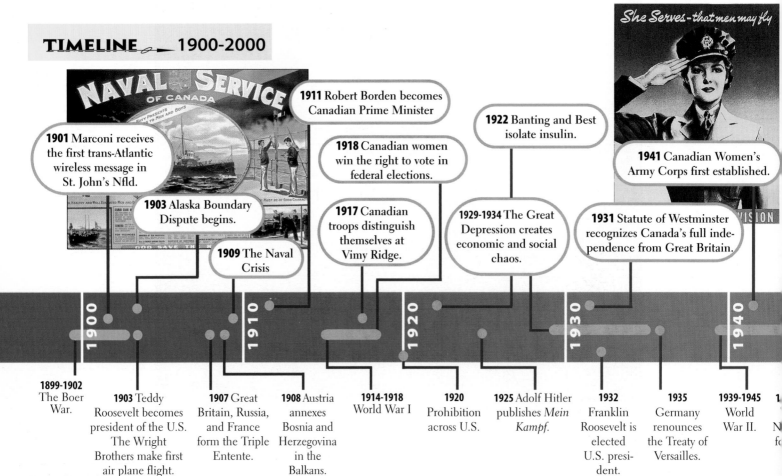

1901 Marconi receives the first trans-Atlantic wireless message in St. John's Nfld.

1903 Alaska Boundary Dispute begins.

1909 The Naval Crisis

1911 Robert Borden becomes Canadian Prime Minister

1917 Canadian troops distinguish themselves at Vimy Ridge.

1918 Canadian women win the right to vote in federal elections.

1922 Banting and Best isolate insulin.

1929-1934 The Great Depression creates economic and social chaos.

1931 Statute of Westminster recognizes Canada's full independence from Great Britain.

1941 Canadian Women's Army Corps first established.

She Serves—that men may fly

1900 — 1910 — 1920 — 1930 — 1940

1899-1902 The Boer War.

1903 Teddy Roosevelt becomes president of the U.S. The Wright Brothers make first air plane flight.

1907 Great Britain, Russia, and France form the Triple Entente.

1908 Austria annexes Bosnia and Herzegovina in the Balkans.

1914-1918 World War I

1920 Prohibition across U.S.

1925 Adolf Hitler publishes *Mein Kampf.*

1932 Franklin Roosevelt is elected U.S. president.

1935 Germany renounces the Treaty of Versailles.

1939-1945 World War II.

As well, at the turn of the century Canada was peaceful. The drums of war that beat so insistently in Europe were completely muffled in the large expanses of this young country that stretched from sea to sea.

Yet Canada *would* become intimately involved in two great wars and other serious challenges in the 20th century. The country would also leave the shelter of the British Empire to forge its own destiny as an independent nation. Later, isolation would be replaced by involvement on a global scale. This book offers a brief introduction to Canada's role in global affairs throughout the 20th century. It also challenges you to think about how that role may change in the 21st century.

StatScan	Arrivals in Canada Selected Groups, Selected Years			
Nationalities	**1901**	**1905**	**1909**	**1913**
British	11 810	65 359	52 901	150 542
Austrian	228	837	1 830	1 050
French	360	1 743	1 830	2 755
Spanish	4 702	6 926	6 644	497
Italian	4 710	3 473	4 228	16 601
Japanese	6	354	495	724
Russian	1 044	1 887	3 547	18 623
Swedish	485	1 847	1 135	2 477
U.S.	17 987	43 543	59 832	139 009

Source: Adapted from Canada Year Book, 1913.

During the early part of the 20th century, most immigrants to Canada came from Europe and the United States. Canada's immigration policies actively discouraged immigrants from Asia and even Blacks from the U.S. Canada's doors were not as wide open as they appeared to be at first sight.

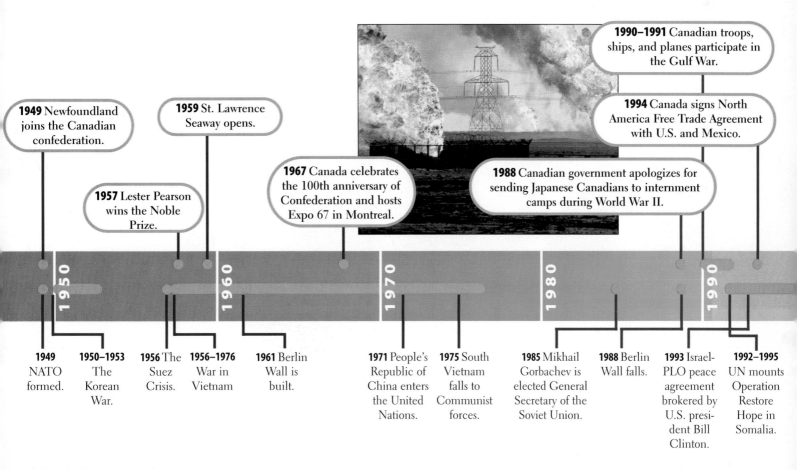

1949 Newfoundland joins the Canadian confederation.

1957 Lester Pearson wins the Noble Prize.

1959 St. Lawrence Seaway opens.

1967 Canada celebrates the 100th anniversary of Confederation and hosts Expo 67 in Montreal.

1988 Canadian government apologizes for sending Japanese Canadians to internment camps during World War II.

1990–1991 Canadian troops, ships, and planes participate in the Gulf War.

1994 Canada signs North America Free Trade Agreement with U.S. and Mexico.

1950   1960   1970   1980   1990

1949 NATO formed.

1950–1953 The Korean War.

1956 The Suez Crisis.

1956–1976 War in Vietnam

1961 Berlin Wall is built.

1971 People's Republic of China enters the United Nations.

1975 South Vietnam falls to Communist forces.

1985 Mikhail Gorbachev is elected General Secretary of the Soviet Union.

1988 Berlin Wall falls.

1993 Israel-PLO peace agreement brokered by U.S. president Bill Clinton.

1992–1995 UN mounts Operation Restore Hope in Somalia.

Turn-of-the-Century Thinking

Every historical period has its own set of dominant ideas or beliefs. At the turn of the century, many people in Canada held to the following beliefs:

imperialism: the policy of gaining control over other countries through trade, diplomacy, or war. As an imperial power, Great Britain had control over Canada and other countries in the British Empire.

militarism: the acceptance of war and military force as a necessary way of resolving conflicts and asserting national pride.

nationalism: exaggerated patriotism and the willingness to vigorously pursue national goals without regard to how this will affect other countries.

Can you tell why beliefs like these might lead a country into war?

Imperialism under Fire

The British Empire at the turn of the century formed a network of colonies, dominions, protectorates, and territories that circled the globe. Many Canadians were proud to be part of such a powerful empire. In 1899 when war broke out in the British colony of South Africa, Britain requested the help of its other colonies in fighting the **Boers**.

Most English Canadians felt it was Canada's duty to help Great Britain in the Boer War. Many French Canadians, however, felt that the war in South Africa was none of Canada's business. Liberal Prime Minister Laurier had to seek a compromise between these different views of Canada's role in the British Empire. His solution was to raise and train a volunteer army to serve in South Africa under British control. This compromise pleased few, but it avoided a more bitter and divisive debate in Canada.

The Empire Calls Again—The Naval Bill

As the great empires of Europe began to arm and prepare for war, British military leaders worried about the strength of the rapidly expanding German High Seas Fleet. Since Britain used the Royal Navy to protect international sea lanes, it was natural that Britain would ask Canada to shoulder some of the costs of naval defense.

Some Canadians wanted to send money immediately to Britain for the purchase of battleships. Other Canadians feared getting entangled further in Britain's imperial concerns.

Laurier tried once again to effect a compromise. In 1909 he decided to establish a small Canadian navy to protect Canadian shores but which would also be available to assist Britain in times of crisis. In 1910 the Naval Service Act was passed and two ships, the Niobe and the Rainbow, were purchased from Great Britain.

This solution satisfied neither group. Canadian imperialists felt such a tiny "tinpot navy" was an insult to Britain. Canadian nationalists, particularly in French Canada, felt this navy was too small to be an effective defense. They also thought that by placing it under British control, Canada would still be dragged into future wars that posed no direct threat to North America.

Figure 1-2 Canadian Nursing Sister Minnie Affleck with several of the wounded soldiers in South Africa. A number of Canadian women served overseas as nurses during the Boer War. Many more would follow in their footsteps during World War I.

Figure 1-3 Recruitment poster for the young Canadian navy.

MAP STUDY   THE ALASKAN BOUNDARY DISPUTE

The Alaskan Boundary Dispute

N

0   200   400 km
Scale

ALASKA

• Dawson City

Yukon R.

YUKON TERRITORY

Chilkoot Pass

PACIFIC OCEAN

BRITISH COLUMBIA

Prince of Wales Is.

Queen Charlotte Islands

.... Trail of '98
———— US claim
- - - - - - Canadian claim
— ·· — Boundary (1903)

In 1903 Canada and the United States found themselves in a serious disagreement over the location of the border between Canada and Alaska. American president Teddy Roosevelt pursued his nation's claim to the disputed territory with great energy. Canadian leaders were less aggressive in pursuing their claims. Because Great Britain still oversaw Canadian affairs, British imperial concerns were important in resolving the dispute. At this time Britain was very concerned about the rising threat of Germany's military might and did not want to alienate the U.S., a potential ally. For this reason, Britain supported the U.S. claim over Canada's, and in 1909 the territory became American. This is one example of a case in which Canadian nationalism finished second to British imperialism.

The practical result of Laurier's compromise was that when war *did* break out in 1914, Canada had a navy of two aging, barely seaworthy vessels, with crews numbering less than 400 officers and men. Competing nationalisms and on–going debates about Canada's role in the British Empire meant that the navy was neither able to defend Canada nor to assist Great Britain.

Laurier was defeated in the election of 1911 by Robert Borden's Conservative Party. The quiet optimism of 1900 would soon be swept away by the forces of nationalism, imperialism, and militarism that erupted in World War I. Laurier's golden vision for the 20th century would be replaced by the stark realism of his successor's world view.

Figure 1-4 Robert Borden won the election of 1911 largely as a result of widespread dissatisfaction with a series of compromises brokered by Sir Wilfrid Laurier. Many Canadians were still unhappy with Laurier's Naval Bill. Also, there was a great deal of opposition to the Reciprocity Treaty, which would allow manufactured goods from the United States into Canada with sharply lowered tariff rates. Canadian manufacturers felt that these imported goods would provide unfair competition to their own. Nationalists in Canada fuelled anti-Laurier sentiments by claiming that Canada would soon become a colony of the U.S. if the Treaty was approved.

> **The world has drifted far from its old anchorage and no man can with certainty prophesy what the outcome will be.**
> —Prime Minister Robert Borden, in 1914

RECONNECT

1. In your own words describe imperialism, nationalism, and militarism.

2. Do these ideas still motivate people and nations in the world today? Explain.

2 The Road to War

> **FOCUS**
>
> This section will help you understand
> a. the major reasons for the outbreak of World War I
> b. why Canada became involved in World War I.

TIMELINE 1900-1920

1900 — French Canadian students riot for three days in Montreal, protesting Canada's involvement in the Boer War.

1903 — Canadian commissioners refuse to sign the document ending the Alaska Boundary Dispute. The agreement takes force anyway after signing by British and American commissioners.

1905 — Alberta and Saskatchewan become provinces in the Dominion of Canada.

1910 — Quebec nationalist leader Henri Bourrassa begins publishing *Le Devoir*. Its first issue blasts the naval policy of Prime Minister Wilfrid Laurier.

1911 — In the federal election, Robert Borden's Conservatives unseat Wilfrid Laurier's Liberals.

1914 — Canada enters World War I on the side of Britain and France.

1915 — Canadian troops fight in their first major battle of the war, when the Germans attack Ypres with chlorine gas.

1916 — The Newfoundland Regiment is wiped out at the Battle of the Somme.

1917 — Canadian troops capture Vimy Ridge.

The Conscription Crisis divides Canada along French-English lines.

1918 — The Armistice ends the war in Europe.

1919 — Sir Wilfrid Laurier dies.

The Treaty of Versailles is signed.

1920 — Canada joins in founding the League of Nations in Geneva.

Robert Borden resigns as Canadian Prime Minister.

The Causes of War

Even today historians are still arguing about the causes of World War I. There is little agreement over which nation or group of nations was most to blame for actually starting the war. There *is* broad agreement, however, over why the nations of Europe were ready for a war and why, once the war started, so many of them were drawn into it.

As we have already seen, nationalism, imperialism, and militarism were all popular ideals at this time. Together they had the effect of preparing people psychologically for the idea that war was inevitable. Two other political trends of the time also help to explain how the war got started. These trends were:

▶ the eagerness with which individual countries entered into **alliances** with each other, and

▶ the rise of **terrorism**.

Alliances

All the major powers in Europe at this time eventually settled into two alliances whose members pledged to support each other in time of war. These alliances had the effect of encouraging conflict because each nation knew it could rely on its allies for help. The first alliance was called the Triple Entente and consisted of Great Britain, France, and Russia. Opposing the Triple Entente was the Triple Alliance, which consisted of Germany, Italy, and Austria-Hungary. Most of the other countries in Europe had ties to one or the other of these two groups.

MAPSTUDY — EUROPE IN 1914

Triple Entente
Triple Alliance
Neutral Nations
Joined Triple Entente
Joined Triple Alliance

Note: In 1915, Italy joined the Triple Entente

Using the map to the left, answer the following questions.

1. Which nations became allies of the Triple Entente?

2. Which nations became allies of the Triple Alliance?

3. What appear to be the geographic advantages of each alliance?

4. What happened to Italy once the war started?

Terrorism and the Black Hand

Several political groups in Europe at the turn of the century used terrorism to achieve their goals. They targeted monarchs, generals, and prime ministers for assassination. The frequency and bloodiness of terrorist bombings horrified Europeans. The most spectacular of these assassinations occurred in a remote corner of Europe and proved to be the spark that ignited all-out war.

Archduke Franz Ferdinand, heir to the Austrian throne, and his wife Sophia were visiting the Austrian province of Bosnia in the **Balkans**. Bosnia, which had been annexed by Austria-Hungary in 1908, was a hotbed of nationalist sentiment. There were many Serbs living there who wanted to free Bosnia from Austrian domination. A small group of Bosnian Serbs formed a terrorist organization called the Black Hand. They warned that if Franz Ferdinand came to Bosnia, they would kill him.

When Franz Ferdinand and his wife set out to tour Bosnia's capital Sarajevo, the Black Hand stationed several assassins along the route. After a reception at the town hall, the motorcade was returning to the governor's palace when Franz Ferdinand and Sophia were both gunned down by Gavrilo Princip, a nineteen-year-old student.

Austria-Hungary issued an **ultimatum** demanding that Serbia allow its forces to enter the country to search for the assassins. Serbia refused and was supported by Russia. Germany promised to help Austria-Hungary, and Russia asked France for help. In August 1914 Germany invaded Belgium, and this pulled Great Britain into the conflict. World War I had begun.

Figure 2-1 Gavrilo Princip assassinates Archduke Franz Ferdinand and his wife Sophia. Princip was unrepentant about the killings. "No, I am not sorry. I have cleaned an evil out of the way."

RECONNECT

1. Summarize in your own words the major causes of World War I.

Over There: The Canadian Expeditionary Force (CEF)

FOCUS

This section will help you understand
  a. how a Canadian army was created on short notice to fight in World War I
  b. the uneasy relationship that developed between Canadian soldiers and British officers.

Seeing Action

In 1910, well before the start of World War I, Prime Minister Wilfrid Laurier observed, "When Britain is at war, Canada is at war. There are no distinctions." By 1914 Canada was still far from being an independent nation. Even though we ran our own domestic affairs, our foreign policy was still supervised by Britain. Canada had no legal authority either to declare war or to make peace. We shared the British flag and the British monarch. The first telegrams informing Ottawa of the declaration of war came from Britain's Colonial Office! To the mother country, Canada was still a loyal colony that did what it was told.

Once the war began in August 1914, the biggest concern for many Canadians was to get a taste of the action before the war ended. For many people,

the thought of war was exciting and romantic. Most were sure it would be over by Christmas. The German **Kaiser** Wilhelm II promised his troops, "You will be home before the leaves have fallen from the trees."

British Officers

Sir Sam Hughes, Canada's Minister of Militia, had made a point of enlisting citizen soldiers and officers for the Canadian Expeditionary Force (CEF) instead of professional career soldiers. He was convinced that a citizen army would make a better fighting force. Their amateur status and lack of training meant that the majority of Canadian soldiers were unused to military discipline. British officers, on the other hand, were often drawn from the

---

TIMELINE — **The Creation of the Canadian Expeditionary Force**

August 4, 1914	Great Britain declares war on Germany, and Canada enters the war on Britain's side.
August 5, 1914	The Canadian government orders the enlistment and mobilization of 21 000 soldiers.
August 12, 1914	Minister of Militia Sir Sam Hughes announces that at least 100 000 Canadians have volunteered for military service.
Sept. 10, 1914	By this date, 30 000 troops and 8 000 horses have been assembled at the training camp in Valcartier, Que.
Sept. 23, 1914	The troops leave Valcartier to board ships that will take them to England.
October 3, 1914	The troop convoy leaves Gaspe, Que. for England.
October 4, 1914	The convoy stops to pick up a regiment of Newfoundland volunteers. At this time Newfoundland was still a separate British colony. This regiment would be wiped out in a 40-minute attack on German lines during the Battle of the Somme in 1916.
October 14, 1914	The Canadian troop convoy arrives in England.
February 1915	Canadian troops take up positions around Ypres, Belgium.
	Minister of Militia Sir Sam Hughes had completed one of the most amazing feats of the war: raising, training, equipping, and transporting a new Canadian army of 32 000 soldiers in just over two months.

Figure 3-1 Canadian soldiers marching past Stonehenge in England, 1914. The Canadian army camped on Salisbury Plain, near Stonehenge, and there received further training under British officers. The British at first wanted to break up the Canadian forces and feed them piecemeal into existing British units. Sam Hughes resisted this idea vigorously. In the end, the Canadian troops remained together but while they were in England they were placed under the command of a British officer, Lieutenant-General Edwin Alderson. For the next three months, Alderson put the Canadians through a rigorous program of marching, trench digging, and rifle and bayonet practice.

upper classes. Many of them had already spent years in uniform. They demanded unquestioning respect from their men and expected snappy salutes. Many Canadian soldiers were slow to salute the British officers. They also refused to recognize the class distinctions that were taken for granted in Britain.

The result was predictable. Although the British generally admired the strength and endurance of the Canadian troops, they complained bitterly about their lack of respect and discipline.

By February 1915 Canadian troops had finished their training in England and taken up positions at the **Front**. They dug in beside British **Tommies** in the last narrow corner of Belgium still held by Allied forces. They found themselves near an obscure town called Ypres, a name that would soon become a byword for the horrors of modern warfare.

CultureLink

THE SONGS OF WORLD WAR I

At the beginning of the war, when the troops headed off for the trenches they could often be heard singing. They sang to keep their spirits up and because they had no clear idea of what they were about to encounter. After the bloodshed at the Battle of the Somme in 1916, little singing was heard at the Front. The most popular song of World War I was "Tipperary," but Canada also contributed songs to the war effort.

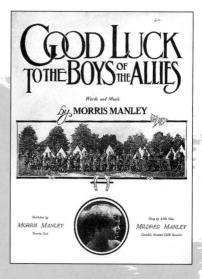

Figure 3-2 Canadian composer Morris Manley quickly produced the popular tune "Good Luck to the Boys of the Allies" soon after the start of World War I.

RECONNECT

1. Identify the most important reason for Canada entering World War I.

2. Explain in your own words why tensions developed between the Canadian and British forces.

FOCUS

This section will help you understand
  a.   why trench warfare was such a terrible experience for the troops in World War I
  b.   some advances in weapon design that took place during the war.

Stalemate

The first few months of the war, between August and November 1914, saw rapid advances by the German army through Belgium and into France. By the time winter arrived, the German advance had stalled and the Front, the line separating the opposing forces, was clearly established. Soldiers on either side dug in behind barbed wire and machine-gun posts in a labyrinth of trenches that slashed across Europe for hundreds of kilometres.

Conditions in the Trenches

Living in the front-line trenches was a constant struggle for survival. Snipers were always a threat, some of them accounting for hundreds of kills. Soldiers did not just fight against the enemy, but also against the cold, the wet, and the mud. Conditions were so bad during the winter that most fighting came to a halt. Major offensives were planned each year for the spring and summer.

Figure 4-1 The night before a raid, a company of soldiers usually went out to cut the enemy's barbed wire. Wide openings had to be made. Otherwise the attacking soldiers would all bunch together at the gaps in the wire, making easy targets for the enemy's machine-gunners.

EyeWitness

Looking for a Cushy

Given the conditions in the trenches, it was not surprising that many soldiers looked for a way out. They began to envy their comrades who had the luck to get a **blighty** or a **cushy**, terms describing a wound serious enough to put them in hospital but not so bad that it would cause lasting damage. In his 1929 memoir, *Good-bye to All That*, British author Robert Graves described the fate of one fellow in his unit who went looking for a cushy.

"A bloke in the Munsters once wanted a cushy, so he waves his hand above the parapet to catch **Fritz's** attention. Nothing doing. He waves his arms about for a couple of minutes. Nothing doing, not a shot. He puts his elbows on the fire-step, hoists his body upside-down and waves his legs about till he gets blood to the head. Not a shot did old Fritz fire. 'Oh,' says the Munster man, 'I don't believe there's a damned square-head there. Where's the German army to?' He has a peek over the top—crack! He gets it in the head. *Fini*."

The squalor of the trenches resulted in thousands of soldiers suffering from **trench foot** and **trench mouth**. They were also infested with head and body lice. At night the rats came out to feed on the garbage, the corpses, and even on some of the sleeping soldiers.

Shell shock was a medical condition first diagnosed during World War I. Some Allied officers thought that shell-shocked soldiers were merely shirking their duties out of cowardice. These genuinely ill soldiers sometimes faced imprisonment, physical abuse, and even firing squads. Canadian doctors early in the war accepted shell shock as a valid psychological illness. They became skilled at diagnosing, documenting, and treating this new condition.

New Weapons
The Machine-Gun

The machine-gun was the definitive weapon of World War I. It gave defenders in an entrenched position a previously unheard of killing efficiency. It was largely because of the machine-gun that the war developed into a stalemate, where neither side could advance against the other. Soldiers often referred to this weapon as the "coffee grinder" because it ground to pieces any group of attackers within range.

The Tank

Figure 4-3 The tank was a British invention whose use was supported by First Lord of the Admiralty Winston Churchill. Most army officers resisted its introduction. Lt.-Gen. Julian Byng once described the tank as "a useful accessory to the infantry, but nothing more." The tank was introduced at the Battle of the Somme in 1916, when about a dozen of the machines were used to no great effect. In 1917, however, 400 tanks broke through the German lines at Cambrai while suffering unusually light casualties. In the last Allied push of the war, in 1918, a formation of 500 tanks swept everything before it and contributed to the collapse of the German line and the end of the war.

The widespread use of the tank in World War II was the main reason there was no repetition of the trench warfare that defined World War I.

Figure 4-2 This is an artist's diagram of the Vickers Mark 1, the standard machine-gun used by the English army in World War I. This gun could fire 550 rounds per minute, making it capable of stopping cold an infantry attack across open ground.

RECONNECT

1. List three reasons why so many soldiers were killed or wounded during World War I.

2. Explain why the tank effectively put an end to trench warfare.

FOCUS

This section will help you understand
  a. the significant role played by authors, musicians, and visual artists in winning and commemorating World War I.

The Art of Propaganda: Lord Beaverbrook

One of the most enthusiastic supporters of the Allied cause was a Canadian named Max Aitken. After making a fortune in the newspaper business, Aitken was named a peer of the British realm and given the title Lord Beaverbrook. He moved to England, won election to the British Parliament in 1910, and became a Cabinet minister during the war.

A man of unusual energy, Lord Beaverbrook assigned himself the task of organizing a group of prominent writers into a highly effective and unofficial ministry of **propaganda**. This top-secret group included some of the most popular and respected writers of the time, among them H.G. Wells, Edith Wharton, Henry James, and G.K. Chesterton.

These writers agreed to collaborate with the British government even to the extent of bending the truth. The group was particularly successful in influencing public opinion in the United States, which was neutral in 1914 but finally did enter the war in 1917. It was only well after the war had ended that the existence of this group became widely known.

CultureLink

H.G. WELLS ON THE ART OF PROPAGANDA

The ultimate purpose of this war is propaganda, the destruction of certain beliefs, and the creation of others. It is to this propaganda that reasonable men must address themselves.

—H.G. Wells, 1914.

Figure 5-1 After World War I, Lord Beaverbrook (in civilian suit) went on to become one of the wealthiest and most influential newspaper tycoons in England. During World War II, he was named Minister of Aircraft Production.

Allied Propaganda

Titles of books written under the umbrella of Lord Beaverbrook's propaganda effort include:

- *Canada in Flanders* by Max Aitken (Lord Beaverbrook)
- *The Old Front Line* by John Masefield
- *His Last Bow* by Arthur Conan Doyle
- *When Blood Is Their Argument* by Ford Maddox Hueffer
- *The War That Will End War* by H.G. Wells
- *Barbarians in Berlin* by G.K. Chesterton

The Canadian War Memorials Fund

Lord Beaverbrook also organized commissions for visual artists to visit the battlefields and record what they saw there. From 1916 to 1919 more than 80 artists from various countries were paid through the Canadian War Memorials Fund to produce 800 works of art. Many of these paintings and sketches are now housed either in the Canadian War Museum in Ottawa or in the British War Museum in London.

Figure 5-2 The Stretcher Bearer Party, by Cyril Henry Barroud. In this painting the artist tried to recreate the desolation and stillness of the battlefield after a day of furious combat.

CultureLink

A POET AT THE FRONT

The Canadian poet Robert Service was an ambulance driver during World War I. By then he was already one of Canada's most popular poets. His fame rested principally on his poems about gold miners in the Yukon, especially "The Cremation of Sam McGee" and "The Shooting of Dan McGrew." Following is his account of transporting a badly wounded soldier from the Front to a field hospital. What is the cruel "twist" in this poem?

A Casualty

The lad I took in the car last night,
    With the body that awfully sagged away
And the lips blood-crisped, and the eyes flame bright,
    And the poor hands folded and cold as clay—
Oh, I've thought and thought of him all day!

For the weary old Doctor says to me:
    "He'll only last for an hour or so,
Both of his legs below the knee
    Blown off by a bomb ... So please go slow,
And bear in mind, lad, he doesn't know."

So I tried to drive with never a jar,
    And there was I cursing the road like mad,
When I hears a ghost of a voice from the car:
    "Tell me old chap, have I copped it bad?"
So I answers "No," and he says, "I'm glad."

"Glad," says he, "for at twenty-two
Life's so splendid, I'd hate to go.
There's so much that a chap might do
And I've fought from the start, and I've suffered so,
T'would be hard to get done in now, you know."

"Forget it," says I, then I drove awhile,
And I passed him a cheery word or two;
Be he didn't answer for many a mile,
So just as the hospital hove in view,
Says I: "Is there nothing that I can do?"

Then he opens his eyes and smiles at me;
And he takes my hand in his trembling hold;
"Thank you—you're far too kind," says he;
"I'm awfully comfy—stay ... let's see:
I fancy my blanket's come unrolled—
My feet, please wrap'em—they're cold ... they're cold."

Source: Originally published in Maclean's Magazine, *March 1918. Reprinted February 27, 1995.*

RECONNECT

1. How did artists and writers help to win the war?

2. What lasting contribution did these artists make?

FOCUS

This section will help you understand
   a.   the high price Canadians paid in their first major battle of World War I.

A Frightening New Weapon

Canadian soldiers received their baptism of fire in one of the most terrible battles of World War I. Near the small Belgian town of Ypres, Canadian and French-Algerian forces held a bulge in the Allied line that the German army surrounded on three sides. The Germans had planned for some time to iron out this bulge. To help them do so they used a weapon that had never before been tested in battle.

On April 22, 1915 German technicians along four miles of the Front opened the valves on 5730 canisters of chlorine gas. The gas formed a huge yellowish-green cloud that drifted slowly over the ground to the Allied trenches. Behind it came 100 000 German troops. The appearance of the gas cloud alone had the effect of terrorizing the Allied troops. As the cloud descended on the trenches, soldiers grabbed their throats, fell to the ground, and were seen "to roll about like mad dogs in their death agonies."

French troops faced the heaviest concentrations of the gas and began to flee from their trenches. This left a large gap in the Allied lines that the Germans immediately smashed through.

Even though the Allied command had been warned that a gas attack was imminent, they had not equipped their troops with gas masks or warned them to take precautions. The soldiers had to improvise. Canadian medical officers advised the men to soak their handkerchiefs in urine and hold them over their faces. This caused the gas to crystallize and neutralized its effect.

The Canadian troops were able to hold their trenches and even extended their lines to close the gaps left by the retreating French. They were the only troops to lead a successful counterattack at Ypres, and the only force to hold their position after being gassed. The Canadians paid a heavy price for their heroism. By the time they were relieved by British troops three days later, more than 6000 Canadians had died.

The German gas attack became known as the second battle of Ypres. Altogether, the town was the site of three major battles during the war. More than 250 000 Allied soldiers were killed in these attacks. Today Ypres is ringed by 140 cemeteries, most of them filled with dead from World War I.

Figure 6-1 Richard Jack's painting shows the fury and desperation of Canada's first major battle in World War I, at Ypres, Belgium. In spite of being gassed and badly outnumbered, Canadian soldiers still managed to stall the German advance.

EyeWitness

Private George Bell

In the confusion of attack and counter-attack, trench raids, gas, and night fighting, the individual soldier often found himself in hellish conditions. Here one soldier describes his involvement in a skirmish at Ypres.

"Forward," command our officers ahead of us. We keep on going. Ahead of me I see men running. Suddenly their legs double up and they sink to the ground. Here's a body with the head shot off. I jump over it. Here's a devil with both legs gone, but still alive. A body of a man means nothing except something to avoid stumbling over. It's just another obstacle. There goes little Elliot, one of the boys from the print shop where I worked in Detroit, only ten yards from me. Poor devil. There's nothing I can do for him. What's one man, more or less, in this slaughter?

— Private George Bell

Source: Daniel G. Dancocks, Welcome to Flanders Fields *(Toronto: McClelland & Stewart, 1989), p. 200.*

On the other side of the lines, a German soldier reflected on the way the war's horror endured long after the battle was over.

The battlefield is fearful. One is overcome by a peculiar, sour, heavy, and penetrating smell of corpses. Rising over a plank bridge you find that its middle is supported only by the body of a long-dead horse. Men that were killed last October lie half in swamp and half in yellow-sprouting beet fields. The legs of an Englishman, still encased in **puttees**, stick out into a trench, the corpse being built into the **parapet**; a soldier hangs his rifle on them.

— Anonymous German soldier.

Source: J. McWilliams and R.J. Steel, Gas! The Battle for Ypres, 1915 *(St. Catharines: Vanwell Press, 1985), p. 206-207.*

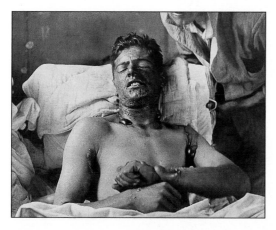

Figure 6-2 Thousands of Canadians were injured by or died from gas attacks in the war. Even though some gassing victims survived the war, they died later as a direct result of the damage to their lungs. This soldier is suffering from both internal and external burns from mustard gas.

Figure 6-3 French-Algerian troops retreat at Ypres. International agreements like the **Geneva Conventions** banned the use of poisonous gas on the battlefield, but both Allied and German forces ignored these restrictions. Today there are also agreements banning the use of poison gases, but many nations still have them in their armouries.

RECONNECT

1. Why is Ypres called Canada's "trial by fire" in World War I? Be specific in your answer.

2. The Geneva Conventions are designed to ensure that modern warfare is conducted in as humane a manner as possible. Do you think a "humane" war is a real possibility?

FOCUS

This section will help you understand
a. why Vimy Ridge was an important objective for the Canadian army
b. why this battle helped to shape the national identity of Canada.

The Attack

At dawn on Easter Monday in 1917, a blinding storm of sleet and snow swept the Douai Plain in France. Vimy Ridge loomed high over the plain like a fortified castle. Strategically, the ridge controlled a large part of occupied France. Packed with thousands of German troops dug in behind miles of barbed wire, it was honeycombed with trenches and machine-gun posts. Seven miles long, the ridge had withstood repeated attacks by French and British troops, costing the Allies more than 200 000 casualties. Vimy Ridge had earned its reputation as an impregnable stronghold.

At 5:30 a.m., 938 artillery pieces on the Allied side set up a **creeping barrage** that worked across the plain and up the face of Vimy Ridge. Usually artillery barrages lasted for days before the troops dared to attack. Not today. Forty thousand Canadian troops followed close behind the exploding shells and up the ridge into the German trenches.

They were in the enemy's face before he could recover from the shelling. Fighting as a unit for the first time in the war, the Canadian troops took command of the ridge within hours. They seized more guns (54 artillery pieces, 104 trench mortars, and 124 machine-guns), took more ground (60 square kilometres), and captured more prisoners (4000) than any British offensive to that point.

Figure 7-1 Canadian soldiers examining a skull unearthed during the fighting at Vimy Ridge. The skull is a macabre reminder that the ridge was the scene of numerous battles long before the successful Canadian assault in 1917.

CaseStudy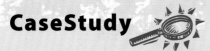

THE PLAN OF ATTACK

The Canadian victory was largely the result of careful planning on the part of British General Julian Byng and the Canadian commander of the First Canadian Division, Major-General Arthur Currie. They realized that the old **tactics** had to change if they wished to take a well-fortified position like Vimy Ridge. Currie, in particular, was a fanatic for leaving nothing to chance. "Thorough preparation must lead to success," he said. "Neglect nothing."

The first stage of Currie's plan involved reconnaissance raids by ground troops and a series of aerial photographs of Vimy Ridge taken from fighter planes. Soon the Canadian Corps knew the position of most of the German troops, artillery, and machine-guns and were able to build accurate scale models of the entire ridge. Each unit then carefully studied its assignment and knew exactly what would be expected of it on the day of the attack.

Behind the lines, construction crews built light railways that would move the artillery for the creeping barrage. In front of the lines, other units were assigned the tasks of cutting the German barbed wire and digging trenches in no man's land that the attacking troops could use for cover. On the day of the attack, the Canadians had the advantage of surprise, partly because they followed so closely behind the barrage, and partly because of the sleet storm and the fact that it was a Christian holy day.

Figure 7-2 Canadian soldiers walk past one of the scale models of Vimy Ridge prior to their attack. Why would a model like this be helpful for the Canadian Corps to have before the battle?

Vimy Ridge was also the first time the entire Canadian Corps fought together as a unit. This seemed to bolster the fighting spirit of the troops. Four Canadians won the **Victoria Cross** for their deeds at Vimy. The Corps' victory was a tremendous morale booster, both for the troops at the Front, and for the Canadian public at home. The cost of victory was high, however. The Canadian Corps suffered more than 10 000 casualties, 3600 of whom died.

EyeWitness

Views of the Battle

From the dugouts, shell holes, and trenches, men sprang into action, fell into artillery formations, and advanced to the ridge, every division of the Corps moved forward together. It was Canada from the Atlantic to the Pacific on parade. I thought then, and I think today, that in those few minutes I witnessed the birth of a nation.

—Brigadier-General Alex Ross, describing the attack.

You could look right down for miles into a beautiful, fertile plain ahead of you—Douai plain—and that's where we saw all the German army just moving. It was the most magnificent sight you ever saw. Horses rushing in, hooking up to the guns, tearing off across the fields to get out of there.

—Sergeant-major Chris Scriven, describing the German retreat as viewed from the top of Vimy Ridge.

We tried to identify some of the boys, to try to get their identity discs off them. But we couldn't do it. See, the boys were blown to pieces, lots of them.

—Corporal Fred Maiden, describing the aftermath of the battle.

RECONNECT

1. Explain in your own words why the Canadian troops were victorious at Vimy Ridge.

2. Why was the battle so important for Canada?

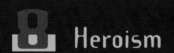
The Meaning of Heroism

Heroism is usually defined as putting one's courage into action. Many soldiers were motivated not so much by the desire to win a particular battle as to save fallen comrades. They often put their own lives at risk while doing so. Tragically, the greatest awards for heroism, such as the Victoria Cross, were often awarded **posthumously**. Following are some profiles of Canadian heroes from World War I.

EyeWitness

The Friendly Giant

Before going to war, Jeremiah Jones was known as "the Friendly Giant" to people in Truro, Nova Scotia. German forces at Vimy Ridge saw a different Jerry Jones in the heat of battle. In 1995, the *Toronto Star* profiled Jones and offered the following summary of his actions.

Jones, a 56-year-old private in the Royal Canadian Regiment, crossed the bloody battlefield at Vimy Ridge and took an enemy machine-gun nest.

His action was heroic for more than the obvious reasons—not only had he contributed to one of the great victories of World War I, the humble giant had proven a Black man's worth in a White man's army.

"I threw a hand bomb right into the nest and killed about seven of them," Jones recalled years later. "I was going to throw another bomb when they threw up their hands and called for mercy."

The hulking 6 1/2 footer ordered the half-dozen survivors out of their hole, then marched them at bayonet-point back to Allied lines, carrying their weapon with them. He had them deposit it at the feet of his commanding officer.

"Is this any good?" he asked.

On August 17, 1917, Jones was celebrated in his hometown newspaper as "a patriot, brave, powerful, and resourceful." His commander recommended him for a Distinguished Conduct Medal, the second-highest valour award after the Victoria Cross.

But the "lion of the hour" was Black, and to give a Black man a bravery medal in 1917 would have been a political bombshell at a time when the military's top brass—and some of the country's senior politicians—had opposed Black enlistment.

Source: Adapted from the Toronto Star, *November 11, 1995. Stephen Thorne, Canadian Press.*

Figure 8-1 Jeremiah Jones.

The Youngest Winner of the Victoria Cross

Many of the Canadian soldiers were teenagers. By lying about their age, some were able to enlist at a younger age than the law allowed. One of these boys, Tommy Ricketts of Newfoundland, became the youngest soldier to win the Victoria Cross in World War I.

Rickets joined the army in 1916 when he was still 14 years old. He entered the front lines in 1917 and was wounded in 1918. Near the end of the war, his unit was pinned down by withering fire from German machine guns. Without any artillery support, the 17-year-old attacked by himself and outflanked the enemy position. He soon drove the gunners off and helped his unit to advance without casualties and to capture the German guns and take prisoners.

When the war was over, Tommy Ricketts returned to Newfoundland and became a pharmacist. When he died in 1967, he was given a state funeral.

The Deadliest Shot in the Army

Aboriginal soldiers were an effective part of Canada's forces in World War I. Many were highly skilled riflemen who proved their worth at Ypres and throughout the war. Francis Pegahmagabow, known as "Peg" to his comrades, was considered "the most dangerous man in the Canadian army." Born into the Caribou clan at Shawanaga, Ontario, "Peg" was awarded the military medal with two bars for his skill as a sniper and scout in some of the toughest battles of the war. He became Canada's most decorated Native soldier to survive the war. As a sniper, he reportedly hit nearly 400 Germans.

After the war Pegahmagabow was twice elected chief of the Ojibwa band at Parry Island, Ontario. He stoutly defended the treaty rights of his people against any inroads by the government or private individuals.

Figure 8-2   Francis Pegahmagabow, one of the deadliest snipers in the Canadian army.

Firing Squads

Not all soldiers were heroes or treated as such. One of the most chilling activities that took place behind the lines was the court-martial of soldiers for criminal activity, cowardice, or negligence. During World War I, 25 Canadian soldiers were executed by firing squads.

Although a number of them had committed serious crimes such as murder, some were executed because they refused to fight, threw away their weapons, fell asleep on duty, or struck an officer. One Canadian soldier was shot because he had been visiting a French girlfriend and reported late for duty.

The executions were usually carried out by firing squads of 12 fellow-soldiers, one of whom was given a blank cartridge. In this way each soldier could hope it was not he who shot his comrade. Some of the condemned soldiers were too terrified to face being blindfolded and tied to a pole before being shot. "If you were lucky," said one soldier later, "your friends got you drunk, or the medical officer gave you an injection. Then you were carried to a chair, tied down, and shot."

RECONNECT

1. Write out your own definition of heroism. To illustrate your definition, provide examples of people you think acted in heroic ways.

FOCUS

This section will help you understand
a. the development of the first air war in history
b. the vital role played by Canadians in that war.

TECHLINK

THE DEVELOPMENT OF THE FIGHTER PLANE

In the opening days of World War I, airplanes were used mainly for **reconnaissance** purposes. Pilots flying over enemy lines would report on troop movements and fortifications. Then a Dutch aircraft designer, Anthony Fokker, developed a synchronizing gear system that allowed a pilot to fire a machine gun through the plane's propeller without hitting the blades. The fighter plane was born.

Later technical developments included sophisticated bombsights, air-cooled and water-cooled engines, and increasing speed, range, and bomb capacity. This new form of combat created an entirely new industry. In Germany alone, 140 different types of flying machines were designed during the war, and 50 000 aircraft were manufactured.

Figure 9-1 This painting by Canadian war artist G.W.R. Nevinson shows a dogfight in progress between Allied and German fighter planes. A pilot became an **ace** after shooting down five enemy aircraft. Canada had four aces with more than 50 "kills," while Germany had three, Great Britain and France two apiece, and the U.S. none. Overall there were 127 Canadian aces with more than 1500 kills among them.

Figure 9-2 A Zeppelin goes down in flames. These airships were first used for scouting purposes, but design changes gradually allowed them to fly farther and higher. The Germans used them in bombing raids that terrorized the citizens of London. German air raids killed 1413 people in Great Britain and injured another 3408. British air raids in Germany killed 720 people and injured 1754. A Canadian pilot was the first to shoot down a Zeppelin.

The Black Flight

In the first half of 1917, German aircraft dominated the skies over the Western Front. Then in June of that year, a small group of Canadian pilots led by Raymond Collishaw began to take control from the Germans. The Canadians called their group the Black Flight. They painted their aircraft black and gave them names like Black Maria, Black Roger, and Black Death.

On June 6, 1917, the Black Flight shot down 10 German airplanes, an event that signalled the end of German control of the skies. In the next two months, the Black Flight flew mission after mission and amassed the unprecedented total of 87 kills against two losses.

CaseStudy

THE RED BARON'S LAST STAND

Both Canadian pilot Roy Brown and the German ace-of-aces Manfred von Richthofen were 25 years old when they met over France in April 1918. By this time, von Richthofen had taken on the status of a living legend, both in Germany and abroad. He had 80 kills to his credit, more than any other pilot in the war. As well, he had taken command of a squadron that had not recorded a single plane shot down and pushed it to the point where it often accounted for more than 20 kills a day. But the constant grind of leading his Flying Circus into battle was wearing the Red Baron down.

On the other side, Roy Brown was relatively unknown, though he had shot down 11 German aircraft. Brown was afflicted with stomach ulcers but continued to fly in spite of constant pain. On the day in question, Brown was flying with a rookie pilot to one side of him. He told Wilfred "Wop" May that he was only to observe that day and not take part in any of the fighting that might develop.

When the two squadrons met, a huge aerial battle developed with more than 50 **dogfights** in progress at once. May soon found himself pursued by a red Fokker triplane. It was the Red Baron, homing in for his 81st kill.

May put his plane into a dive and headed for home. Flying just above the ground of No Man's Land, his plane was soon peppered by bullets from von Richthofen's guns. This time, however, the tired German ace had made a dangerous error. He was so engrossed in hunting his prey he failed to notice that Roy Brown was now on his tail. The Red Baron was also taking ground fire from Australian troops in the trenches. Bullets ripped through the pilot's seat, and Germany's greatest ace was dead at the controls before his plane crashed behind enemy lines.

Germany was stunned at the loss of a favourite son. Morale among the troops and the public plunged even lower. The Allies gave von Richthofen a full military funeral and set above his grave a cross fashioned from two propellers. Even in the midst of the savagery of war, a touch of chivalry survived in these honours granted to a fallen foe.

Figure 9-3 Manfred von Richthofen, Germany's Red Baron. "I think of war as it really is," he said, "not as the people at home imagine, with a Hurrah! and a roar. It is very grim."

Figure 9-4 Canadian pilot Roy Brown once remarked, "I love flying, not killing."

RECONNECT

1. What evidence can you list to demonstrate that Canadian flyers were very skilled pilots?

FOCUS

This section will help you understand
a. the danger posed by German U-boats
b. the role that Canada played in the war at sea
c. the devastation caused by the Halifax Explosion in 1917.

The U-Boat Threat

As soon as the war started, Britain announced a blockade of all German ports. Germany responded with the U-boat, the deadly submarine that preyed on convoys of British ships in **wolf packs**. On May 7, 1915, the luxury liner *Lusitania* was sunk by a U-boat off the coast of Ireland. About 1200 civilians drowned, including 100 Canadians. For many, the destruction of a passenger ship carrying hundreds of women and children came to symbolize the brutal desperation of modern warfare.

Figure 10-1 A British ship, torpedoed by a German U-boat, has turned on its side and is about to sink. When ships were torpedoed, casualties were usually heavy.

In February 1917, Germany announced a policy of "unrestricted submarine warfare." This meant that German U-boats would attack any ship they encountered, enemy or neutral, battleship or hospital ship. The German high command hoped this policy would choke off Britain's critical supply lines to the countries in her global empire.

At one point Britain was reduced to six weeks of food. During the worst phase of unrestricted submarine warfare, 25% of the ships leaving British ports were sunk. By war's end, the U-boats had sent 5408 Allied vessels to the bottom of the ocean. By contrast, the Germans lost 178 U-boats during the course of the war.

StatScan
The U-Boat's Impact on British Shipping

Year	Merchant Shipping Lost (in tonnes)
1914	218 770
1915	776 140
1916	1 122 670
1917	3 382 915
1918	1 537 178

Why was 1917 such a horrible year for British shipping?

Source: Adapted from John Ray, The First World War *(London: Heinemann, 1975), broadsheet 10: "The U-Boat War."*

Canada's Naval Role

The Naval Bill of 1910 first established the Royal Canadian Navy. Since ship construction was a slow process, Canada bought many naval vessels from Britain or converted merchant ships to war ships.

During the war, Canada transported vast quantities of men and supplies to the Allied war machine in Britain and Europe. As the U-boat threat increased, Canada and Britain organized a Canadian Patrol Service to protect shipping between the two countries. Canadian vessels began to serve as "sheep dogs" for convoys of ships headed for Great Britain. By April 1918, Allied losses dropped to 1% of shipping.

The Halifax Explosion

As the war ground on, the port of Halifax became the most important link between the farms and factories of Canada and the European battleground. Almost all of the Canadian production sent to Europe at this time passed through Halifax before making the dangerous journey across the North Atlantic. In spite of its importance to the war, Halifax itself was spared any firsthand experience of the tragedy until December 6, 1917.

On that date, two Allied ships, the *Imo* and the *Mont Blanc*, collided in Halifax harbour. The

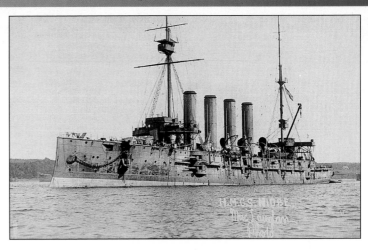

Figure 10-2 The Canadian warship Niobe. When the war began in 1914, Canada had two warships with 359 officers and men. By 1918 there were 112 Canadian warships with 5500 officers and men.

Mont Blanc, loaded with 2400 tonnes of high explosives, turned into a gigantic cannon. It discharged an explosion that was the largest single detonation in history until the dropping of the first atomic bomb on Hiroshima at the end of World War II.

The explosion flattened the city of Halifax and tossed whole ships out of the harbour onto dry land. The immediate death toll stood at 1630, and another 9000 were injured, many of them mutilated by flying shards of glass. Six thousand people were left homeless.

CultureLink

"LIKE A MONSTROUS GRENADE"

The steel hull of the Mont Blanc exploded like a monstrous… grenade. It burst into thousands of jagged pieces of shrapnel… knifing into buildings and human flesh. All the sailors trying to make fast a towline were vaporised except one… who was thrown across the harbour and swam to the Dartmouth shore. The exploding fragments riddled the Imo, killing the captain and pilot. The shaft of the Mont Blanc's anchor, weighing half a ton, flew two miles…

One-third of the homes and businesses of the city of 50 000 people were obliterated in a flash, and the wreckage immediately began to burn. In thousands of crushed houses, coal and wood cooking stoves were overturned, setting the splintered wood on fire. Ruptured gas lines instantly ignited. Many who survived the explosion now faced a more terrible death, trapped in houses that were on fire.

Source: Robert Macneil, Burden of Desire *(New York: Dell Publishing, 1992), pp. 22–24.*

RECONNECT

1. How did Canada participate in the naval war during World War I?

2. Describe the results of the Halifax Explosion.

FOCUS

This section will help you understand
  a. an often overlooked aspect of Canada's history during World War I
  b. the conditions faced by men and women in the internment camps.

The War Measures Act

When the war broke out in 1914, thousands of Canadians expressed their love for their country by volunteering to die for it. At the same time, people were encouraged to hate the enemy. Unfortunately, many people decided that the enemy included Canadians who had emigrated from Germany, Austria-Hungary, and Turkey. The result was that more than 8000 Canadians were rounded up and sent to internment camps. The majority of the people interned, about 6000, were from Ukraine, which was then part of the Austro-Hungarian empire.

These were the very same people the government had enticed to move to Canada in the great period of immigration during the early years of the 20th century. The government had promised them free land,

political freedom, and a bright future. These fellow-Canadians were now classified as **enemy aliens**.

One of the first steps Prime Minister Robert Borden's government took after the war began was to pass a new law, the War Measures Act. This law granted the government sweeping powers to suspend the legal and political rights of Canadian citizens. In regard to "enemy aliens," the government took the following measures:

▶ forced them to register with their local police department and report on a regular basis,

▶ banned the publication and distribution of books and magazines in "enemy" languages, and

▶ sent 8597 enemy aliens to work in remote labour camps for the duration of the war.

Figure 11-1 Rather than live by themselves after their husbands were sent to the internment camps, 81 women agreed to live with their menfolk in the camps. This photo from 1915 shows a group of Ukrainian women and children at the Spirit Lake Camp in northern Quebec, near what is today called La Ferme.

Conditions in the Camps

In Quebec and Ontario, government agents rounded up and transported internees to half-built camps in the remote northern forests. In the western provinces, internees were sent to work on road crews in the new national parks. Many men were sent to the camps simply because they were unable to find work in their hometowns. Others lost the jobs they did have because their employers and co-workers refused to associate with the "enemy."

Conditions in the camps were harsh. The men had to work 10 hours a day, six days a week, and were paid 25¢ a day. (The lowest rank of soldier in the CEF was paid five times this amount.) They were usually cold, tired, depressed, and poorly fed and clothed. They spent their days building roads, clearing brush, and constructing bridges.

The men who were set to guard the internees were themselves poorly equipped and inadequately trained. Some of the guards were still suffering from the shell-shock they had endured in the trenches of Europe. To protest against the camps, internees organized slow-downs, strikes, and escapes. Some of them committed suicide. In a camp at Kapuskasing, Ontario, a full-scale clash erupted between the 1200 prisoners and their 300 guards.

Figure 11-2 Many Canadians might be shocked to learn that this is not a photograph of a German concentration camp during World War II, but of a Canadian labour camp for "enemy aliens" during World War I. The majority of the prisoners at this camp were Canadians of Ukrainian descent.

In an official report, the Northwest Mounted Police noted that, "the closest investigation has not revealed the slightest trace of organization or concerted movement amongst the alien enemies."

CONNECTIONS

INVOKING THE WAR MEASURES ACT

The War Measures Act was first passed by Parliament in 1914. Since then, it has only been invoked three times. In each of these cases controversy over its use continues to the present day.

1. *World War I* The act was invoked to permit the arrest and detention of "enemy aliens," most of whom were of German and Austrian descent. More than 8500 people were rounded up and sent to work in labour camps under harsh conditions. The government never compensated any of these people for their suffering.

2. *World War II* More than 16 000 Japanese Canadians were taken from coastal settlements in British Columbia and moved inland to work camps in B.C., Alberta, and Manitoba. Their land, houses, and businesses were confiscated and sold and their owners received between 5% and 10% of their value in compensation. In 1988 survivors of the internment camps were given a formal apology and a lump-sum settlement of $20 000 each by the government of Canada.

3. *Quebec Hostage Crisis, 1970* After the Front de Liberation du Quebec kidnapped the British trade commissioner and a Quebec cabinet minister, Prime Minister Pierre Trudeau invoked the War Measures Act. Some critics still charge that the act was used more to suppress political protest in Quebec than to head off a violent insurrection.

RECONNECT

1. What actions did Canada take against so-called enemy aliens during World War I?

FOCUS

This section will help you understand
  a. how Canadians at home participated in the war effort.

Feeding the Troops

Since the war had turned much of the agricultural land of Europe into battlefields of mud and blood, the pressure was on Canadian farmers to supply the troops with grain, dairy, and meat products. Canada was the closest and most productive of Britain's overseas colonies, so it was logical for the mother country to call on Canadians for help. With demand skyrocketing, produce prices rose and the farm economy boomed.

The only problem on the farms was that with so many young men in uniform, harvesting the crops was difficult. Canadians responded to the challenge in a variety of ways:
▶ women from the city and the country served as "farmerettes,"
▶ civil servants and teachers gave up their vacations to help bring in the crop, and
▶ students were given time off school during the harvest season.

The Munitions Industry

Canada had virtually no munitions industry in 1914 and few factories capable of producing rifles, bombs, and shells. The first weapons produced in Canada were shoddy, expensive, and late in the delivery. The British complained vociferously that they had signed $170 million worth of war contracts but only received $5 million worth of material.

Government leaders organized the Imperial Munitions Board to improve production. Canada's munitions industry grew from next to nothing to a busy network of 600 factories with 250 000 employees supplying $2 million worth of munitions a day. A whole new industry was created, one that would form the basis for Canada's industrial network for years to come.

StatScan
Canadian War Production

Year	Value of War Materials Produced
1914	$28 164
1915	$57 213 688
1916	$296 505 257
1917	$388 213 553
1918	$260 711 751

Figure 12-1 With more hectares brought under the plough and more young men going overseas, bringing in the harvest required an extraordinary effort. Many women became "farmerettes" and worked in the fields as these women did at Souris, Manitoba. As the war continued, farmers used more machinery to make up for the loss of human labour.

CaseStudy

WAR PROFITEERING

Although the outbreak of the war was a tragedy for many Canadians, for a few business people it was an opportunity to rack up huge profits. Canadian business leaders were called upon to supply vast amounts of food, materials, and weapons to Britain and the United States, as well as for the war effort at home.

Sir Joseph Flavelle was a multimillionaire **entrepreneur** and philanthropist. Before the war he owned the largest meat packing company in the British Empire. During the war he ran the Imperial Munitions Board and proved to be a tough but capable leader who successfully upgraded Canada's wartime production.

In the meantime, though, Flavelle's meat packing company quadrupled its profits in the first year of the war. People criticized Flavelle as a **war profiteer**. They accused him of driving up the price of pork by stockpiling huge quantities until the price rose so high he could sell his stock at a great profit. Although Flavelle was later exonerated, the damage to his reputation was permanent.

The Borden government responded to the public outcry against war profiteers by passing two new taxes into law. The first was on business profits and the second was a "temporary" tax on income. The income tax is one of the most enduring legacies of World War I. It continues today to be a major source of revenue for both the federal and provincial governments.

Figure 12-2
A 1917 cartoon shows Joseph Flavelle standing by pork barrels filled with money. William Davies was the name of Flavelle's meat packing company. What is the artist suggesting about Flavelle's activities during the war?

Paying for the War

Canada found itself mired in a depression at the beginning of World War I, so funding the largest enterprise in Canadian history was a great challenge. Canada's defence bill soared from $13 million in 1914 to $311 million in 1918. Money owed to Great Britain for CEF expenses reached a high of $252 million. The money to pay all these bills came from three sources: loans, donations, and eventually taxes.

Canadians of all ages contributed to a host of charities aimed at helping soldiers' families, providing packages for men at the front, and building and supplying hospitals. Women were especially active in the **Canadian Patriotic Front**, and even children could buy **Victory Stamps** to help pay for the war.

When the government turned to Canadian citizens in 1915 with the first of its **Victory Bond** campaigns, it hoped to raise $50 million. Citizens responded to such an unexpected degree that $100 million poured into government coffers. Each new Victory Bond campaign was greeted with the same enthusiastic response.

Figure 12-3
Businesses and private individuals responded to the government's repeated Victory Bond drives by buying more than $1 billion worth of the bonds over the course of the war. Posters like these were a common sight during the war.

RECONNECT

1. What sort of work done by Canadians at home do you think was most important in supporting the war effort?

2. In your view, should business people be allowed to make large profits during a war? Why or why not?

FOCUS

This section will help you understand
  a. the essential role played by women in World War I
  b. how World War I permanently changed conditions for women in Canada.

> **If women in war factories stopped for 20 minutes, we should lose the war.**
> —General Joseph Joffre, French Commander-in-Chief

On the Home Front

War had traditionally been viewed as a male "contest," too savagely violent for the participation of women. During World War I, the resistance against acknowledging the abilities of women was gradually set aside. This happened partly because women joined the workforce in larger numbers than ever before to replace the men who had gone to fight. During the war, Canadian women participated in a host of activities that aided the Canadian cause. Among other things, they

▶ replaced men in banks, factories, offices, schools and transportation centres.

▶ formed the nucleus of the workforce in the new war munitions industry.

▶ raised millions of dollars for the war effort and the support of soldiers' families.

▶ managed farms and harvested crops.

▶ made thousands of dressings for battlefield wounds.

▶ organized knitting clubs and sent warm clothing to the soldiers shivering in the trenches.

▶ sent packages of soap, candy, and cigarettes to the soldiers.

▶ carefully rationed food and manufactured goods so that more products were available to the armed forces.

▶ bore the loss of loved ones and attended to the needs of wounded soldiers.

The Hardest Loss

On a personal level, thousands of Canadian mothers, wives, and daughters bore the terrible pain of losing sons, husbands, and fathers to the war. Many others had to deal with the problems associated with men who did return home but were broken in body or spirit. Some soldiers faced a long and difficult convalescence. Disfigurement and loss of limbs were not easily treated at this time. Also, many families that were deprived of their main salary earner were condemned to years of poverty.

Figure 13-1 More than 30 000 women worked in the munitions industry during the war. Factory work meant a pay packet, new skills, some personal freedom, and pride in contributing to the war effort. Women proved to be excellent workers in these factories, and their dexterity was highly valued. Look carefully at this photograph. Who were the supervisors in this factory?

Figure 13-2 This mother attended the unveiling of the Vimy Memorial in France in 1936. The lines etched on her face hint at the pain she endured in losing eight sons in the war. Their medals adorn her coat.

The Fight for the Vote

By the time World War I began, there had been an active women's **suffrage** movement in Canada for more than 25 years, but women still did not enjoy the right to vote. For the suffragists, the war presented an opportunity to demonstrate the full abilities of women. As more and more women took over positions vacated by men fighting in the war, it became harder to resist the logic of extending the **franchise** to women. Under the continual pressure of suffragists like Nellie McClung, Dorothy Davis, Emily Murphy, and Flora Denison, the walls of resistance began to crumble.

The final push came during the federal election campaign in 1917. Robert Borden's Conservative government was mired in the Conscription Crisis and found its popularity plummeting. Desperate for votes, Borden promised to extend the franchise to women if he was re-elected. His party won the election, and in 1918 the government passed the bill that finally granted Canadian women the right to vote.

TIMELINE — **World War I and Women's Right to Vote**

1916	Manitoba, Alberta, and Saskatchewan grant women the right to vote in provincial elections.
1917	Because of huge numbers of casualties and too few volunteers, the Conscription Bill is introduced to draft more men into the Armed Forces.
1917	The Military Voters Act extends the vote in federal elections to nurses serving in the war.
1917	The Wartime Elections Act extends the vote to wives, widows, mothers, sisters, and daughters of soldiers.
1917	The Conservative government of Robert Borden is re-elected after Borden promises to extend voting rights to all women over 21.
1918	Federal Women's Franchise Act gives the vote in federal elections to all women over 21 who are British subjects.
1920	Women are granted the right to seek election to the House of Commons.
1921	Agnes Macphail becomes the first woman ever elected to the Canadian House of Commons.

Figure 13-3 A funeral with military honours was given to Canadian nurses who died when German planes bombed their hospital. More than 2500 women left Canada to serve as nurses during the war. They endured shelling, aerial bombardment, and the dreadful conditions in the field hospitals. Over the course of the war, 46 Canadian nurses lost their lives.

RECONNECT

1. Outline the connection between World War I and Canadian women winning the right to vote.

2. What role played by women during the war do you think was most important? Why?

FOCUS

This section will help you understand
   a. why **conscription** was introduced in 1917 and what its results were
   b. why this was such a controversial issue in Canada.

> "There has not been and there will not be compulsion or conscription. Freely and voluntarily, the manhood of Canada stands ready to fight beyond the seas.
> —Prime Minister Robert Borden in December 1914.

A Shift in Public Opinion

The quote above would come back to haunt Prime Minister Borden as the war dragged on. After the savage fighting around Ypres in 1915 and at the Battle of the Somme in 1916, it was obvious that the war would be a prolonged, deadly affair. No one had been prepared for the enormous number of the dead. By 1917, the recruiting rates were so low that the Canadian Corps had to send injured soldiers back to the Front before they'd had time to recover from their wounds.

REASONS WHY RECRUITING SLOWED

▶ People no longer thought of the war as a "glorious adventure."

▶ The casualty figures, regularly printed in the newspapers, dampened the public's enthusiasm.

▶ Young men realized that if they went to the Front their chances of survival were slim.

▶ At home, employment and wages were booming.

▶ Farmers across Canada claimed that they needed all available hands on the farm.

StatScan
1917: The Conscription Crisis

Month	Enlistments	Casualties
January	9 194	4 396
February	6 809	1 250
March	6 640	6 161
April (Vimy Ridge)	5 530	13 477
May	6 407	13 457
June	6 348	7 931
July	3 882	7 906
August (Hill 70)	3 117	13 232
September	3 588	10 990
October	4 884	5 929
November (Passchendaele)	4 019	30 741
December	3 921	7 476

Carefully review these statistics on recruitment and casualty figures for 1917. At which month does the Canadian Corps appear to be suffering its greatest crisis?

Figure 14-1 The band of the Canadian Tenth Battalion. The entire band was wiped out by one artillery shell on May 1, 1917. Over the course of the war, 5390 men served in the Tenth Battalion, and 85% of them became casualties. It was this sort of slaughter that led to the Conscription Crisis.

French Canada's Response

Although French Canadians supported the war initially, few did so with enthusiasm. Of nearly 500 000 volunteers over the course of the war, only about 13 000 were French speaking. French Canadian units distinguished themselves during the war, particularly the 22nd regiment, the famed Van Doos. Two French Canadian soldiers won the Victoria Cross. In general, however, the French viewed the army and its recruiters as an English organization. Also, French anti-war sentiment was aggravated by a continuing conflict over French language rights in schools in Ontario and Quebec.

Borden's Gamble

By 1917 Borden knew something had to be done immediately to enlarge the CEF. He also knew that the length and savagery of the war made it a source of conflict among all Canadians. Borden took several steps to try and resolve the crisis.

▶ He approached Liberal leader Wilfrid Laurier with the idea of forming a "union" government, free of the old political divisions. Laurier refused because he, like most French Canadians, opposed the idea of conscription. Borden did succeed, however, in persuading many English-speaking Liberals to support his government.

▶ In July 1917, Borden's government passed the Military Service Act (MSA), which allowed the government to draft civilians into the army for overseas service.

▶ To increase his chances of re-election, Borden forced two more bills through the House. The Military Voters Act extended the vote to all members of the armed forces, both male and female. This meant that women who worked as nurses or ambulance drivers for the CEF could vote in federal elections.

▶ The Wartime Elections Act gave the vote to mothers, wives, daughters, and sisters of men serving overseas. This controversial law also denied the vote to conscientious objectors and naturalized Canadians born in enemy countries.

Most of the new voters supported Borden because they thought conscription would help end the war sooner. Borden crushed Laurier at the polls. Unionist forces won 153 seats to Laurier's 82. In Quebec, however, Borden received only 3 seats to Laurier's 62. French-English division over conscription was complete.

Borden got the new soldiers he so desperately needed. The MSA produced 100 000 new conscripts, 25 000 of whom went overseas before the war ended. In Quebec, anti-conscription riots broke out in which four civilians were killed and 10 soldiers wounded.

Figure 14-2 With the passing of the Military Voters Act, these Canadian nurses in France were among the first women to vote in a Canadian federal election. Election results proved Borden was right in his belief that the majority of military voters, whether they were male or female, would support his government in the election of 1917.

RECONNECT

1. In your own words, give three reasons why enlistments decreased as the war dragged on.

2. What would you say was the major result of the Conscription Crisis?

FOCUS

This section will help you understand
a. what the major results of World War I were for Canadians
b. how World War I helped Canada establish its independence from Great Britain.

CROSSFIRE

WAS IT WORTH IT?

Should Canada have participated in World War I? Were the results of the war worth the price paid? Consider the following points and determine for yourself the answers to these questions. You may wish to add other points to either side of the debate.

The Positive Results

▶ Canada was now an equal partner with Britain in world affairs, no longer a mere colony.
▶ Canadians took great pride in the accomplishments of their fighting forces and the people at home.
▶ Canada won international praise for its achievements during the war and for the first time took a prominent position on the world stage.
▶ Canadian industry and agriculture boomed during the war.
▶ Canadian women received the right to vote.
▶ Canada was granted two seats at the peace negotiations that led to the Treaty of Versailles. Canada was also a signatory in its own right to the treaty, not as a colony subject to Great Britain.
▶ Canada won an independent seat with voting rights in the newly formed League of Nations.

The Negative Results

▶ Almost one-third of all Canadian enlistments were casualties during the war. Of these, 61 326 died and 172 950 were wounded.
▶ By the end of the war French- and English-speaking Canadians were bitterly divided over the question of conscription.
▶ Many Canadians were angry about the war profiteering of some business people.
▶ As a result of the War Measures Act, Canadians shipped innocent people to labour camps and lost some basic freedoms to government control during the war.
▶ The income tax became a permanent fixture of Canadian society.
▶ The national debt ballooned from $463 million in 1913 to $2.46 billion by 1918.

Figure 15-1 Adolf Hitler, a corporal in the German army during World War I, is seated on the far right. The bitterness of Germany's defeat and the harsh terms of the Versailles Treaty that followed would lead Hitler to plunge the world into another terrible conflict 20 years later.

BIOGRAPHY

Subject: Robert Borden

Dates: 1854-1937

Most Notable Accomplishment: Borden successfully led Canada through the difficulties of a long and agonizing war. By gaining international recognition for his country's achievements during the war, he helped establish Canada's political independence from Great Britain.

Thumbnail Sketch: Born to parents of modest means, Borden had to work hard to get an education. He became a teacher, then a very successful lawyer. In 1896 he entered politics for the Conservative Party, and by 1901 he was party leader. He worked skillfully to defeat Sir Wilfrid Laurier in the election of 1911. When war broke out in 1914, Borden quickly rallied Canadians to Britain's side. Under his leadership, Canada raised a great army, which by the end of the war was an independent fighting force completely under the command of Canadian officers.

Borden lobbied hard to win Canada a greater share of responsibility for the way the war was waged. It was largely as a result of his persistence that Canada and other Dominions were represented in the new Imperial War Cabinet, which was responsible for planning the war. Borden was instrumental in transforming the British Empire into the British Commonwealth of Nations. He insisted that Canada represent its own interests at the Paris Peace Conference, with the result that Canada was given two seats of its own at the Conference. This in turn led to Canada being given its own seat at the League of Nations when it was established in 1919.

Exhausted by the demands of leading the country through nine of the most difficult years in its history, Borden resigned as Prime Minister in 1920.

Significant Quote: After the disastrous slaughter of Canadian troops at Passchendaele, Borden confronted Britain's Prime Minister David Lloyd George with the following words. "Mr. Prime Minister, I want to tell you that if there is a repetition of the battle of Passchendaele, not a Canadian soldier will leave the shores of Canada as long as the Canadian people entrust the government of Canada to my hands."

Turn-of-the-Century Thinking, Revisited

What became of the three popular concepts that had pushed the world into the "war to end all wars:" militarism, imperialism, and nationalism?

imperialism: The empires of Germany, Austria-Hungary, and Russia were shattered by the war. The French and British still had their empires, but the member nations had begun to clamour for independence.

militarism: The war convinced many former militarists that armed conflict was futile and a terrible waste of human life. At the same time, some countries, notably Germany, produced leaders who thirsted for the revenge that only another war could provide.

nationalism: Among the new countries created from the wreck of the German and Austro-Hungarian empires (such as Czechoslovakia and Yugoslavia) nationalism was an even more vital force than before the war. In Canada too, nationalism remained strong, although French and English Canadians differed over what it meant.

NETSURFER

Three excellent websites for further research on World War I:

1. World War I—Trenches on the Web.
   http://www.worldwar1.com
   • first-rate graphics, interesting text.
   • invites students to research items and help build the site.

2. Lost Poets of the Great War.
   http://www.cc.emery.edu/English/Lost Poets
   • biographies and poetry of the war's greatest poets, including: Wilfrid Owen, John McCrae, Rupert Brooke, and Isaac Rosenberg.

3. Veterans Affairs. **http://www.vac-acc.gc.ca**
   • website for Canada's Department of Veterans Affairs.
   • includes many eyewitness accounts.

RECONNECT

1. In your opinion, what was the most significant result of World War I for Canada? Explain your choice.

2. Was Robert Borden a "great" Canadian Prime Minister? Explain.

16 Between the Wars

FOCUS

This section will help you understand
a. how the peace settlement after World War I paved the way for a future war.

Someday, as a tourist, you may visit Europe. Suppose your plane landed in Paris and you travelled from there to the northeast, towards Brussels in Belgium or Amsterdam in the Netherlands. Along the way you will notice a number of huge cemeteries. All the grave markers are the same: simple white crosses arranged in neat rows that seem to stretch all the way to the horizon. These are the great military cemeteries of World War I, beautifully maintained and usually dominated by a monument commemorating the sacrifice of millions of people in the "war that will end war."

TIMELINE ⌐ 1918-1945

1919	Treaty of Versailles is signed.
1920	League of Nations created.
1921	Mackenzie King becomes Prime Minister of Canada.
1931	Japan conquers Manchuria.
1933	Hitler becomes Chancellor of Germany.
1935	Mussolini invades Ethiopia.
1938	Hitler annexes Austria.
1939	Germany signs non-aggression pact with Soviet Union. Germany invades Poland. Britain, France, and Canada declare war on Germany.
1941	Germany invades Soviet Union, which then joins the Allies. Japanese attack on Pearl Harbor brings U.S. into the war.
1942	Canadian forces raid Dieppe and suffer heavy losses.
1943	Italy surrenders to the Allied forces.
1944	D-Day. Allied armies land on the beaches of Normandy in France.
1945	The United Nations is founded. Germany surrenders. Two atomic bombs are dropped on Japan. World War II ends with the surrender of Japan.

The survivors of that now-distant war promised themselves and their children, "Never again!" This unit will examine how that promise was broken, only 21 years later, by an even more terrible war.

The Treaty of Versailles

The signing of the Armistice on November 11, 1918 in a railroad car in France brought an end to World War I. To the weary survivors, this marked the dawn of a bright new age. A lasting peace was the goal of winners and losers alike when they met at Versailles, just outside Paris, in January 1919. But the delegates from defeated Germany would soon learn that peace could take many forms. They had to face the leaders of the three most powerful countries in the world: Premier Georges Clemenceau of France, Prime Minister David Lloyd George of Great Britain, and President Woodrow Wilson of the United States.

You can see the approach that each of these countries took to the peace process by examining the Peacemakers chart on page 35.

Figure 16-1 The German delegation signs the Versailles Treaty. Watching are the three seated victors, Wilson of the United States, Lloyd George of Great Britain, and Clemenceau of France.

THE PEACEMAKERS

Wilson	Lloyd George	Clemenceau	German Delegation
• wanted a just and honourable peace for Germany based on a plan that came to be known as the **"Fourteen Points."** • favoured self-determination: that all racial and ethnic groups should have the right to choose the country they wished to live in. • advocated disarmament. • would prohibit any more secret alliances. • argued on behalf of establishing the League of Nations.	• favoured a moderate peace with Germany but was forced by British voters to take a harsh stand. • was conscious of heavy British losses during the war and wanted to prevent the future rise of an aggressive Germany.	• France must be avenged by regaining the provinces of Alsace and Lorraine, seized by Germany after the Franco-Prussian War of 1871. • Germany should be crippled so it could never again threaten France.	• Germany surrendered because it felt it would be treated fairly based on Wilson's Fourteen Points. • Germany was not solely responsible for the war. • most Germans would reject a crippling peace, especially the militarists.

THE TREATY OF VERSAILLES

In the end the harsh attitude toward defeated Germany won out. The main points of the Versailles Treaty are outlined below. They pushed Germany into an economic depression that would last into the 1930s.

▶ Germany must pay the costs of the war: $32 billion.

▶ Germany's western border with France, the Rhineland, was to be permanently demilitarized, thus preventing future surprise attacks on France.

▶ The victors seized all of Germany's overseas colonies.

▶ The German coal fields in the Saar valley were to be given to France for at least 15 years.

▶ Germany surrendered one-eighth of its pre-war territory, parts of it going to France, Denmark, Poland, and Czechoslovakia.

▶ The German navy was reduced to a few surface ships, the air force totally abolished, and the army cut to a maximum of 100 000 men.

▶ The "War Guilt Clause" stated that Germany must accept sole responsibility for causing World War I.

Primary Source

MEIN KAMPF

Adolf Hitler had this to say about the Treaty of Versailles:

"These points have been burned into the brain and emotion of this people, until finally in sixty million heads, a common sense of shame and a common hatred would become a single fiery sea of flame, from whose heat a will as hard as steel would have risen and a cry burst forth: 'Give us arms again'."

—from *Mein Kampf (My Struggle)*.

RECONNECT

1. Which of the three Allied leaders had the most influence in drafting the treaty? Who had the least?

2. What emotions was Hitler appealing to in the German people?

FOCUS

This section will help you understand
a. why dictatorships arose in Europe and Asia after World War I
b. how the presence of these dictatorships made World War II inevitable.

Dictators and the League of Nations

The ten years following the signing of the Treaty of Versailles were relatively peaceful and prosperous for the world's major industrial nations. The bubble burst in 1929 when the stock market crash led to the Great Depression. This period of massive unemployment, stagnant trade, and crushing poverty witnessed the rise of a number of dictatorships around the world.

The League of Nations was created in 1919 as a world organization "to promote international cooperation and to achieve international peace and security." Largely the brain-child of U.S. President Woodrow Wilson, the League failed in its stated goal for two reasons. First the U.S., ironically, never joined. Isolationists in the U.S. feared becoming entangled in further European conflicts. Secondly, the League failed to intervene when military dictatorships in Japan, Italy, and Germany seized the territories of weaker neighbours. By the late 1930s, it was obvious that the League was an organization without the power to carry out its goals.

Japanese Expansion in Asia

In 1931 Japan faced severe economic problems that were made worse by a soaring birthrate. The country's military leadership launched an invasion of a mineral-rich area of China called Manchuria. Located just north of Japanese-dominated Korea, this area seemed the ideal solution to Japan's need for more living space.

Despite appeals from the League of Nations to withdraw, the Japanese army continued to occupy Manchuria. The League finally sent a fact-finding mission to Manchuria and condemned Japanese aggression. By that time, however, Japan had taken over all of Manchuria and renamed it Manchuko.

Mussolini's Second Roman Empire

Conditions in Italy following World War I were appalling. From 1915 to 1922, the cost of living increased by 500%. The country was on the verge of revolution when, in 1922, Benito Mussolini and his **Fascist** followers, known as Blackshirts, marched on Rome. In 1925, Mussolini proclaimed himself dictator, Il Duce.

By abolishing democratic government, Mussolini was able to outlaw rival political parties and strikes. Using propaganda and a censored press, he promised a total reform of Italian society and a new prosperity. He was credited with eliminating social chaos and economic inefficiency—he "made the trains run on time." His dream was to restore to Italy the grandeur and might of the Roman Empire.

Mussolini learned a lesson from Japan's invasion of Manchuria. He came to believe that the answer to Italy's problems lay in aggressive expansion abroad. In 1935 Mussolini ordered the invasion of Ethiopia, the only country in Africa that was still independent.

The Ethiopian emperor, Hailie Selassie, made a passionate appeal to the League to intervene. Here again was a naked act of aggression, this time much closer to Europe. The League reacted by branding Italy an aggressor and imposing limited sanctions on goods being traded with Italy.

Although the League reacted, it did not go far enough. Italy was still able to obtain strategic items such as oil.

Figure 17-1
Mussolini delivers one of his fiery speeches to his devoted followers. Why was Mussolini so popular in Italy during the 1920s and '30s?

Later in 1935, W.A. Riddell, Canada's delegate to the League, proposed that all oil shipments to Italy should stop. Without oil for his planes and tanks, Mussolini would have been forced to abandon his campaign in Ethiopia. Prime Minister Mackenzie King overruled Riddell's proposal.

Mussolini's forces crushed Ethiopian resistance with dive bombers and poison gas, while the League stood by and did nothing.

Adolf Hitler and the Rise of Nazi Germany

To a Germany suffering greatly from the Depression, Hitler promised higher wages and living conditions, full employment, and a restoration of the national pride that had been snuffed out by the Treaty of Versailles. In casting about for **scapegoats** he could blame for all of Germany's problems, Hitler began to heap blame on Communists and Jews.

After being named Chancellor in 1933, Hitler withdrew Germany from the League of Nations. This paved the way for his annexation of Austria in 1938 and seizure of part of Czechoslovakia later that same year. The road to war was open.

Figure 17-2 Adolf Hitler at a rally attended by German school children. In what ways were Mussolini and Hitler alike?

EyeWitness

Canadian Prime Minister Mackenzie King met with Adolf Hitler in 1938. He had this to say about the German dictator:

"I believe the world will yet come to see a very great man-mystic in Hitler. Much I cannot abide in Nazism—the regimentation, cruelty, oppression of the Jews. But Hitler himself, the peasant, will rank some day with Joan of Arc among the deliverers of his people, and if he is only careful may yet be the deliverer of Europe."

Source: C.P. Stacey, A Very Double Life, (Toronto: Macmillan, 1976), p. 187.

Primary Source

"Germany's goal cannot be taken without the invasion of foreign states or attacks upon foreign property. I shall give a propagandist cause for starting the war: never mind if it be plausible or not. The victor shall not be asked afterwards whether he told the truth or not."

—Adolf Hitler. Quoted in R.G. Waite, ed., Hitler and Nazi Germany (Toronto: Holt-Rhinehart, 1969), p. 187.

RECONNECT

1. How did the dictatorships respond to the problems of the Depression?

2. How did the League of Nations respond to the military dictators?

FOCUS

This section will help you understand
a. why World War II erupted when it did
b. how Canada became involved in the war.

TIMELINE — The Road to War

1933 As leader of Germany's largest party, Hitler is chosen Chancellor of Germany.

1935 Hitler announces that the German army will recruit more than 100 000 men, the limit set by the Treaty of Versailles.

The people in the coal fields of the Saar Valley, given to France under the Treaty of Versailles, vote overwhelmingly to return to Germany. Britain urges France to be moderate in its dealings with Germany. This policy comes to be known as appeasement.

1936 Hitler orders his troops into the demilitarized zone known as the Rhineland, which forms a border area between France and Germany. The Germans then rebuild the fortifications there, a flagrant breach of the Treaty of Versailles. The League of Nations does nothing.

1938 **August** To fulfill his pledge to unite all German-speaking people under one rule, Hitler annexes Austria. This is known as the Anschluss.

September Hitler demands the return of the Sudetenland, an area given to Czechoslavakia after World War I despite its having a population of 3.5 million German-speaking people. Believing Hitler's pledge that this was his last territorial demand, Britain's Prime Minister Neville Chamberlain signs the Munich Agreement, which hands over the Sudetenland to Germany. The Czechs are outraged, but Chamberlain claims to have secured "Peace in our time."

October Germany and Italy sign "Axis" cooperation pact; Japan joins later. These three nations become known as the Axis Powers.

1939 **March** Great Britain assures Poland it will protect it from German aggression. Hitler demands the return of all "German" territory given to Poland by the Treaty of Versailles.

August 23 Nazi Germany and the Soviet Union sign a Non-Aggression Pact, promising not to wage war on each other. Hitler can now use force on Poland without having to worry about the Soviet Union.

September 1 Hitler orders the invasion of Poland on the pretext that Polish agents were conducting sabotage along the German-Polish border.

September 3 Britain and France declare war on Germany.

September 10 Canada declares war on Germany.

Blitzkrieg

Blitzkrieg is the German word for "lightning war." Its aim was to avoid the stalemate of trench warfare by overrunning a country before it had time to defend itself. The typical attack would begin with the Luftwaffe (the German air force) bombing strategic targets such as air fields and communication centres. Following close behind were the Panzers (tanks) and motorized infantry, which rapidly smashed enemy resistance and occupied conquered territory.

Figure 18-1
British Prime Minister Chamberlain waves the Munich Agreement on his return from Germany, promising it will secure "peace in our time." The Agreement was signed on September 30, 1938. How long did Chamberlain's "peace" last?

In this way, Germany was able to defeat Poland in less than a month, taking more than 700 000 prisoners. Small countries were especially vulnerable to blitzkrieg tactics. In April 1940, Germany overran Norway and Denmark. In May, Holland and Belgium were invaded. Sweeping into the heart of France through Belgium and Luxembourg, the Germans forced the French to surrender in a month.

Deliverance from Dunkirk

By late May 1940, the Germans had forced the British Expeditionary Force and its French and Belgian allies into Dunkirk, the only Channel port in France not yet taken by the enemy. More than 400 000 Allied soldiers were trapped. Fortunately for the Allies, Hitler made his first major blunder of the war. He listened to Reichsmarshal Herman Goering, who claimed that his Luftwaffe would win a quick victory. This set the stage for a miraculous rescue operation.

The British launched "Operation Dynamo." Between May 27 and June 4, a strange assortment of 850 rescue craft picked up more than 338 000 soldiers from the beaches of Dunkirk. Tanks, trucks, and guns were deliberately wrecked and left behind, but the men were saved to fight another day.

Figure 18-2   The front page of Toronto's *Globe and Mail* newspaper on September 11, 1939, the day after Canada declared war on Germany.

Figure 18-3   On June 22, 1940, a jubilant Hitler accepted France's surrender in the same railroad car in which Germany had signed the Armistice in 1918.

Primary Source

PRIME MINISTER CHURCHILL

Winston Churchill, who had succeeded Chamberlain as Prime Minister in May 1940, realized how overwhelming the German victories could seem to the British people. To counteract their effect, he delivered a series of determined speeches in the House of Commons. The following comes from a speech he gave on June 4, 1940, the day the last British soldier was evacuated from Dunkirk.

"We shall go on to the end. We shall fight in France, we shall fight on the seas and oceans, we shall fight with growing confidence and growing strength in the air; we shall defend our island whatever the cost may be. We shall fight on the beaches, we shall fight on the landing grounds, we shall fight on the fields and in the streets. We shall fight in the hills. We shall never surrender."

RECONNECT

1. Hitler promised revenge for the Treaty of Versailles. From the timeline in this chapter, outline how he went about getting it.

2. You are an 18-year old Canadian male or female in 1940. You have read the news headlines of September 11, 1939.

   a. List the emotions you are experiencing, and for each of them give a reason.

   b. Give your opinion. Should Canada be involved in this war? Explain fully.

FOCUS

This section will help you understand
  a. how unprepared for war Canada was in 1939
  b. what the country did to respond to the challenge of war.

Canada's armed forces had been kept small during the 1920s because most Canadians opposed any sort of military build-up during peace time. The Great Depression caused these already small forces to be cut back even further. Total expenditures of the Department of National Defence for the fiscal year of 1932–33 were only $14 million.

In January 1935, the Chief of the General Staff, Major General Andrew McNaughton, prepared a memo entitled *In Defence of Canada* that he presented to the House of Commons. He stated that Canada's defences were almost "non-existent."

Number 242 Squadron

Both British and Canadian politicians were eager to show strong Canadian participation in the war from its earliest stages. One way to do this was to create a Canadian fighter squadron from the more than 1000 Canadians already serving with the **RAF**. On October 30, 1939, the 242 Squadron was born.

Figure 19-1 Once again, Canadian artists became part of the war effort. This painting by Canadian artist Orville Fischer is called "Recruits Wanted, 1941."

After being equipped with **Hawker Hurricanes**, the squadron saw combat during the Dunkirk evacuation and in the skies over northern France. During the Battle of Britain, 242 Squadron was

Primary Source

IN DEFENCE OF CANADA

As regards reserves of equipment and ammunition, there are none, except as regards rifles and rifle ammunition, partial stocks of which were inherited from the Great War. As regards equipment, the situation is almost equally serious. I select a few items from the long lists of deficiencies on file at National Defence Headquarters:

◆ There is not a single modern anti-aircraft gun of any sort in Canada.

◆ The stocks of field gun ammunition on hand represent 90 minutes' fire at normal rates for the field guns inherited from the Great War and which are now obsolescent.

◆ The coast defence armament is obsolescent and, in some cases, defective in that a number of the major guns are not expected to be able to fire more than a dozen or so rounds.

◆ About the only article of which stocks are held are horses, and this is practically useless. The composition of a modern land force will include very little horsed transport.

◆ There are only 25 aircraft of service type in Canada, all of which are obsolescent except for training purposes; of these, 15 were purchased before 1931 and are practically worn out. The remaining 10 were procured in 1934 from the Air Ministry. Not a single machine is of a type fit to employ in active operations.

◆ Not one service bomb is held in Canada.

—*Major General Andrew McNaughton*

commanded by Douglas Bader, a remarkable Englishman who had lost both legs in an airplane crash before the war. Bader learned to walk and fly again and was able to convince the authorities that he could pilot fighter planes.

Like all fighter squadrons, 242 suffered extremely heavy losses. The life expectancy of fighter pilots was measured in weeks. Of the first 25 Canadian pilots, 16 were killed, three became prisoners of war, and two left because of injuries. Among those killed was Willie McKnight, who twice won the Distinguished Flying Cross and shot down 16 enemy aircraft. He was lost over the English Channel in December 1941.

Casualty replacements seldom came from Canada, and in May 1942, at the request of the Royal Canadian Air Force, the Squadron lost its Canadian designation. During the brief history of 242 Squadron, the young pilots, 23 years old on average, had distinguished themselves.

Recruitment of Women

As during World War I, women joined the work force in large numbers, replacing the men who left their jobs to join the armed forces. In World War II, however, women were also aggressively recruited for the armed forces. Starting in July 1941 the different divisions in the Armed Forces created auxiliaries for women who wanted to join up.

Figure 19-2 The men of 242 Squadron early in the war. The legless squadron leader, Douglas Bader, is fourth from the right. Sitting on the wing fifth from the right is the ace Willy McKnight.

Figure 19-3 A World War II recruitment poster for women. Do you think the same kind of poster would be used today? Why or why not?

ENLISTMENTS BY WOMEN IN CANADA'S ARMED FORCES	
Navy	6 665
Air Force	16 221
Army	20 497
Medical Services	4 439
Doctors	58

Figure 19-4 The figures show what a substantial commitment Canadian women made to the Armed Forces during World War II.

WEEKLY WAGES FOR WOMEN	
Live-in domestic servant	$3.50
Eaton's mail order clerk	$12.00
War plant worker	$25.00

Figure 19-5 The figures in this chart show why war plant work was eagerly sought by women during World War II. Even at $25.00 a week, however, they were still making less than men did for the exact same job.

RECONNECT

1. How prepared was Canada for war in 1939?

2. What roles did Canadian women play in World War II?

FOCUS

This section will help you understand
a. why the Dieppe raid took place and why Canadian troops were involved
b. why the casualty rates were so high.

The Allied raid on the French port of Dieppe on August 19, 1942 only lasted nine hours, but they were nine of the worst hours that Canadian soldiers endured during World War II. The raiding party consisted of 4963 soldiers from the Canadian Second Division, 1075 British Commandos, and 50 U. S. Rangers. Of the Canadians, 907 were killed and 1946 taken prisoner.

Why Dieppe?

In the summer of 1942, there were many reasons for the Allies to mount a raid that would test the coastal defences of Hitler's *Festung Europa*, Fortress Europe. The Soviet Union, which Germany had invaded in June 1941, was pressing its Western allies to open a second front. Churchill was hungry for a morale-boosting victory. Canadian troops, some of whom had been training in Britain since September 1939, were clamouring to take part in some real fighting.

Dieppe was chosen as a target because a large fleet could reach it under cover of darkness. It was within easy range of RAF fighter planes, and it would give the Allies experience in carrying out a major **amphibious** assault. The aim was to destroy as many German defences in and around Dieppe as possible: air fields, rail and harbour facilities, and fuel dumps. Then the troops would return to England, taking German prisoners back with them for interrogation.

On August 18, the troops were assembled aboard a fleet of 237 ships. The raiders were scheduled to attack just after dawn, hitting eight beaches across a 16-kilometre front and catching the German defenders napping. The element of surprise was crucial. Dieppe was well-fortified and protected by high bluffs. The actual attack when it came was not well coordinated. Many of the Canadian troops arrived late. After the first wave ran into fierce resistance, the reserve troops were ordered onto the beaches, where they found the Germans waiting for them.

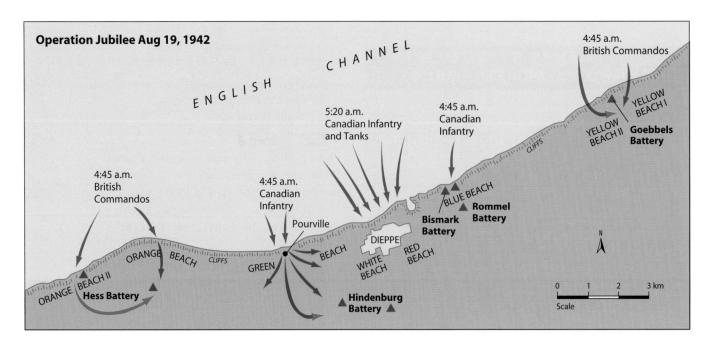

Figure 20-1 As you can see from the map, the British Commandos were assigned the task of knocking out gun batteries on either side of Dieppe, while the main Canadian force bore the responsibility for a direct assault on the fortifications in front of Dieppe. Why is timing such an important factor in an assault of this kind?

Figure 20-2
The slaughter at Dieppe resulted in two-thirds of the Allied forces being killed, wounded, or captured.

The Attack

Orange Beach

Landing under cover of darkness at 4:45 a.m., British Commandos overcame the defenders of a six-gun battery in a furious 15-minute knife and bayonet battle, blew up the guns, and headed back to the beaches with four prisoners.

Yellow Beach

At 3:45 a.m. the British Commandos headed for Yellow Beach ran into a small German convoy, which scattered their forces. Only a third of the troops were able to land one hour later; they failed to knock out the battery; and most were quickly killed, wounded, or captured.

Blue Beach

In a hopeless three-hour fight, the Royal Regiment of Canada suffered 96% casualties. Out of 554 officers and enlisted men, only 65 got back safely to England.

Green Beach

The Canadians quickly overran the town of Pourville. German resistance soon stiffened, however, and the regiments were forced to abandon their objectives.

Main Beaches

The main beaches quickly turned into a terrible killing ground. The Essex Scottish Regiment suffered almost 80% casualties within an hour of landing. The 27 Churchill tanks from the Calgary Tank Regiment made little headway. Some climbed over the sea wall but then ground to a halt before the concrete anti-tank barriers at the entrance to Dieppe. One by one, they were picked off by German anti-tank guns.

Garbled radio messages from shore persuaded Major-General J. H. Roberts to commit his reserves to an already hopeless battle. Believing that an entire regiment had fought their way into Dieppe, not just a handful of survivors, he sent the Fusiliers Mont-Royal to support them. With no cover to shelter them from German guns, this regiment was massacred on the beach.

Meanwhile, in the skies above Dieppe, 67 squadrons of the Royal Air Force (including eight of the Royal Canadian Air Force) fought the Luftwaffe in the single biggest air battle of the war. The Germans decisively beat the Allies here as well, losing 48 aircraft to 106 Allied planes downed.

The Dieppe Raid was a costly disaster for the Allies. Inadequate planning, poor preparation, and the lack of heavy air and naval bombardment all taught a painful lesson in how *not* to attack Hitler's Fortress Europe.

CONNECTIONS

DIEPPE AND D-DAY

Although the raid on Dieppe was a costly disaster, the Allies learned a valuable lesson: trying to seize a heavily defended port by attacking from the sea was unwise. This lesson influenced the Allies' choice of a landing area for the D-Day attack in 1944. The Normandy beaches, although well fortified, did not contain the kind of concentrated defences that surrounded Dieppe. The Allies also learned lessons about timing, air and sea support, and diversionary tactics that had a direct impact on the successful D-Day attack.

The next time Canadian forces attacked Dieppe was in September 1944. They entered the town from the landward side and took it quite easily.

RECONNECT

1. Why did the Allies attack Dieppe?

2. Why were Canadian casualties so high?

FOCUS

This section will help you understand
a. the important role played by the Royal Canadian Navy (RCN) in helping to win World War II.

The War at Sea

When World War II began, the Royal Canadian Navy had only six warships and five minesweepers to protect the country's coastlines. Naval personnel numbered around 2000, about the population of a large high school. A succession of governments had been reluctant to spend money on the Navy. As Canadian Senator Raoul Dandurand stated in 1924, in Canada "we live in a fireproof house far from inflammable materials."

This complacent attitude changed in the spring of 1940 after British and French forces were routed from Europe. This exposed Britain to the threat of invasion by Germany. Now Britain looked to Canada as the source of food, raw materials, and weapons for war.

In order to fight the Battle of the Atlantic effectively, the Canadian government began a crash program of building warships and recruiting people to fight in them. By war's end, the RCN had grown to 373 warships and 93 000 men and women.

The Corvette

The warship chosen to respond to the German U-boat threat was the corvette. Easy and cheap to produce, more than 120 corvettes were built in Canada, each bearing the name of a Canadian city. The corvette was 58 metres long and armed with a cannon, machine guns, and depth charges. The depth charge resembled an oil drum and was packed with about 100 kilograms of explosives set to detonate at a pre-selected depth. They were rolled off the stern of the corvette or catapulted from the sides. If they exploded close enough to a submerged U-boat, the force would crack the submarine's pressure hull, causing it to sink.

At the beginning of the war, corvettes were equipped with a primitive sound-detection system called ASDIC, which could only detect enemy ships when they were submerged. Especially at night, a U-boat could surface and fire its torpedoes undetected by ASDIC. It wasn't until early in 1941 that radar systems were installed in Canadian ships and the war slowly began to turn against the U-boats.

The small, highly manoeuvrable corvettes could bounce over the waves at speeds of 16-17 knots (about 35 kilometres an hour). Living conditions were none too pleasant. To conserve fresh water, showers were forbidden. It took between 10 and 20 days to cross the Atlantic in a convoy. As each day passed, the atmosphere on board the corvette became more and more "ripe." Coupled with this was the ever-present fear that a torpedo would blow your ship apart.

Figure 21-2 Two sailors on a corvette prepare to fire a depth charge, one of the deadliest anti-submarine devices.

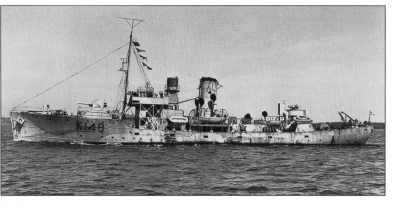

Figure 21-1 Corvettes like this one helped the RCN to destroy a total of 27 enemy submarines during World War II.

The fear was justified. During the first six months of 1942, almost 400 Allied ships were sunk in the North Atlantic while only seven U-boats were destroyed.

E y e W i t n e s s

Torpedo!

Suddenly, like lightning, a colossal flash leapt upward from the convoy. In a moment it resolved itself into a tremendous flame which shot upwards from the water, accompanied by a roar like the passing of an express train. The great column of fire, whose diameter might have been equal to the length of the ship from whose tanks it sprang, seemed almost to reach the cloud base. The whole convoy was lit up by its brilliance: I caught a murmur around me, as of the letting out of breath from many throats.

Then, with equal suddenness, the light went out as though consumed by some fire-eating monster, leaving utter blackness.

But as our eyes became once more accustomed to the darkness, we saw a great black cloud of smoke, like a dense thunderhead, rolling across the sky to leeward—all that was left of a cargo which had until now been destined for the machinery of war on land or in the air.

No one aboard could have survived. I turned away to the westward with a sickening feeling which must have been shared by all who witnessed the attack, except the U-boat commander who fired the torpedoes.

—*Source: Alan Easton, quoted in Heather Robertson,* A Terrible Beauty *(Ottawa: Lorimer, 1977), p. 116.*

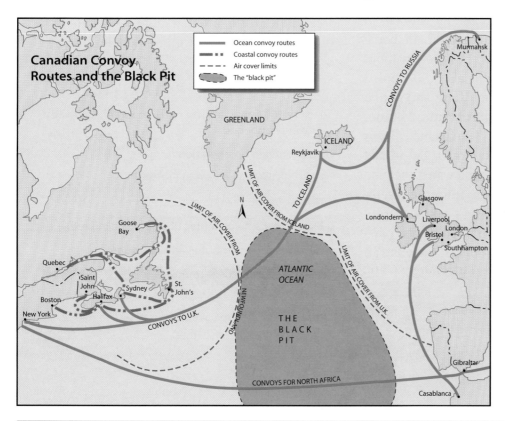

Figure 21-3 The Allies adopted the convoy system early in the war to protect their merchant shipping from attack by enemy submarines and surface raiders. Aircraft could only escort the convoys as far east as 600 miles from Newfoundland, and British planes could protect them on the last leg of their voyage to Londonderry in Northern Ireland. There was no air cover for the vast expanse of ocean known as the Greenland Gap or the "Black Pit." For the first three years of the war, Allied ships were being sunk far faster than they could be built.

RECONNECT

1. List the key ingredients that contributed to the victory of the Royal Canadian Navy in the Battle of the Atlantic.

FOCUS

This section will help you understand
a. how the Royal Canadian Air Force (RCAF) grew from insignificance to the world's fourth-largest air force
b. the role the RCAF played in helping to defeat Germany.

The Royal Canadian Air Force was woefully unprepared for war. When the war started in September 1939, Canada's Air Force consisted of 210 aircraft, only 36 of which were modern combat airplanes. There were just 5000 permanent Air Force personnel. When King George VI and his consort Queen Elizabeth toured Canada in 1939, few realized that their fighter escort was virtually the only air defence Canada possessed.

The British Commonwealth Air Training Plan (BCATP)

In December 1939, the British Commonwealth Air Training Plan was born, which set up schools in Canada to train pilots for Britain's Royal Air Force (RAF). This did not take place, however, without hard bargaining by Canadian officials, who wanted Canadian aircrews to serve in the RCAF and not be incorporated into the RAF. In spite of Prime Minister Mackenzie King's desire for a "Canadianized" Air Force, however, many Canadian airmen did in fact serve with RAF squadrons during the war.

The BCATP turned Canada into the "aerodrome of democracy" and by war's end had produced an amazing number of trained pilots, navigators, radio operators, and gunners, as the chart in Figure 22-1 shows.

Number of flying schools created in Canada	97
RCAF personnel trained	72 835
RAF personnel trained	42 110
RAAF (Royal Australian Air Force)	9 606
RNZAF (Royal New Zealand Air Force)	7 002
Total personnel trained	**131 553**

Figure 22-1 Number of personnel trained by the British Commonwealth Air Training Plan. Canada paid about half of the total costs for the BCATP, which were $607 million. Canadian aircrew served in virtually every combat sector of

The RCAF in Combat

Development of the long-range Lancaster night bomber enabled the RCAF to operate over the whole of Germany. By the beginning of 1943, Allied air forces, including 11 RCAF squadrons, were carrying out massive **saturation bombing** raids over Nazi-occupied Europe. The main targets were the industrial cities in the Ruhr valley, where the giant Krupp armaments factories were located.

From its tiny beginnings in 1939, the Royal Canadian Air Force grew by 1945 to more than 164 000 personnel, including 16 000 women. In six years the RCAF had become the fourth-largest air force in the world, a remarkable achievement for a country of less than 12 million people.

AIRCREW FATALITIES

To every 100 Canadian and British bomber aircrew the following happened:

51%	killed on operations
9%	killed in crashes in England
3%	seriously injured in crashes
12%	became prisoners of war (some injured)
1%	shot down but evaded capture
24%	survived unharmed

Figure 22-2 The typical airman had less than 4 to 1 odds of surviving the war unscathed.

the war, from the Aleutian Islands to North Africa, from Burma to Western Europe. For every Canadian who flew, 15 more were required to service aircraft on the ground.

Figure 22-3 RCAF fighter planes at an airfield in England. Fighter pilots had to "scramble" to intercept German bombers before they reached Britain. A fast response time was critical. Douglas Bader, the legless British ace, was usually airborne within two minutes of receiving the order to scramble.

Figure 22-4 Collecting the dead after the fire bombing of Dresden. The vast majority of those killed were civilians.

CROSSFIRE
THE MORALITY OF SATURATION BOMBING

Many historians have criticized the saturation bombing by the Allies of German cities like Berlin, Hamburg, and Cologne. Particularly unnecessary, they say, was the fire bombing of Dresden on the night of February 13-14, 1945. The city had no military importance and was swelled with refugees near the war's end. No one knows exactly how many people were killed in the raid, but estimates range between 35 000 and 135 000, most of whom were civilians.

"Our crew was involved in the bombing of Dresden, but I can't remember the raid being that spectacular or talked about too much until after the war finished. A large number of German civilians were involved in the German war machine and that's what we were trying to smash. If we killed German factory workers who worked in a shoe factory rather than a munitions plant, then we were preventing shoes from reaching the German fighting forces."

—Bernie Wyatt, *Maximum Effort*, p. 153.

Another Canadian airman who was on one of the 66 Canadian planes that took part in the destruction of Dresden had this to say:

"I participated in the Dresden affair, which was a terrible thing. The fire raid. I understand there were about 135 000 or so people killed in that raid. You didn't need any atomic bombs; you could create what is called a firestorm. You had incendiaries and then heavy bombs, and this would create an artificial wind roaring up the streets and it sucked the oxygen out, and people didn't die of fire: they died because the life was literally sucked right out of them."

—Barry Broadfoot, *Six War Years*, p. 269.

RECONNECT

1. How did Canada contribute to the air war during World War II?

2. In your view, should Canadians have participated in saturation bombing raids? Explain fully.

FOCUS

This section will help you understand
a. that Canadians had to live with many wartime rules and restrictions
b. why, during World War II, Canada endured another Conscription Crisis.

Canadians do not think of themselves as having an especially "military" society. In times of peace, the Canadian Armed Forces are usually quite small compared with the armies of some other nations. During World War II, however, Canadian society was transformed. Even civilians—men, women, and children—submitted to a host of rules and restrictions on their lives, working long and hard to defeat the enemy. During this period, virtually every aspect of civilian life was under government control.

As a Canadian citizen, you were always conscious of your duty to help the war effort. If you picked up a newspaper or turned on the radio, you were blitzed with appeals to your patriotism: join the Armed Forces, take a job in a war industry, buy Victory Bonds, grow a Victory Garden, give blood, watch what you say in case an Axis spy is lurking nearby.

Canada was insulated from the worst effects of the war by the Atlantic and Pacific oceans. No Canadian city was bombed as London was. No Canadian children starved to death, as children in Leningrad did. And despite rationing, Canada's people were well clothed and well fed.

Figure 23-1 Groceries that we take for granted today were subject to rationing during World War II. Coffee, tea, and sugar became luxury items before the war was over. Note the warning: "Loyal citizens do not hoard." Why do you think the government wanted to discourage hoarding?

Rationing

So many resources were being used by the Armed Forces or sent as supplies to Britain or Russia, that shortages soon developed. In April 1942, the Wartime Prices and Trade Board (WPTB) was created to supervise the rationing of various materials. Rationing was an attempt to ensure that every Canadian got a fair share of available supplies.

Gasoline was the first commodity to be rationed. Before long the program was extended to include weekly rations, per consumer, of one kilo of meat, 250 grams of sugar, 250 grams of butter, 30 grams of tea, and 115 grams of coffee.

Consumers were issued ration books containing pages of coupons. These had to be torn off in front of the store clerk as you bought the supplies to which you were entitled.

STATSCAN

What Canadian Workers Produced for the War Effort

- 16 000 aircraft
- 741 naval vessels (plus 3302 landing craft)
- 410 cargo vessels
- 800 000 transport vehicles
- 50 000 tanks
- 148 000 heavy guns
- 2 million tons of chemicals and explosives
- 133 million rounds of heavy ammunition
- 5 billion rounds of small-arms ammunition
- uniforms and supplies for the entire Armed Forces

Source: Department of Munitions and Supplies.

Figure 23-2 During the war, Canadian kids had to give up reading full colour American comics. Instead they read black-and-white magazines like *Canadian Heroes*. The synthetic dyes used in comic books could be put to better use in the war effort.

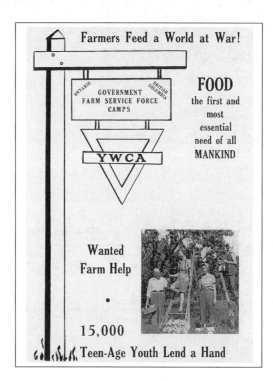

Figure 23-3 Posters like this urged teenagers to participate in the war effort by working on Farm Service Camps. Students of all ages were encouraged to "do their bit." They took part in recycling drives, collecting paper, rags, metal, rubber, and bones. Some even gave away their toys for metal salvage drives. They bought war savings stamps by the millions, knitted socks and scarves for soldiers, and wrote letters to prisoners of war.

BIOGRAPHY

Subject: Clarence Decatur (C.D.) Howe

Dates: 1886–1960

Most Notable Accomplishment: By mobilizing Canada's workforce behind the war effort, C.D. Howe turned the country into a major industrial power on the world stage.

Thumbnail Sketch: C. D. Howe was appointed Minister of Munitions and Supply in April 1940, a job of immense power and responsibility. Howe's energy, persuasiveness, and ability to make important decisions quickly made him equal to the demands of the new position. He enlisted some of Canada's top industrialists to work in his ministry at the salary of one dollar a year.

Figure 23-4 C.D. Howe.

Howe and his team set to work to mobilize Canada's entire industry and workforce behind the war effort. They secured the fuel and supplies necessary, and they allocated the workers needed to make Canada's factories models of productiveness.

In his ruthless pursuit of ever-higher production figures, Howe made many enemies. They called him "Dictator" Howe and "Minister of Everything." Yet his wartime achievements were undeniable. Under his direction, Canadian workers churned out the weapons of war in enormous numbers. Never in Canadian history has one person controlled the lives of so many workers and executives and changed Canadian society so much and so quickly.

Significant Quote: Born and raised in New England, Howe came to Canada at the age of 22 and later described himself as "an American by birth, a Canadian by choice."

Conscription Again

The question of conscription, or compulsory military service, haunted Mackenzie King's government throughout the war. The Prime Minister had a very clear memory of the bitter feelings conscription had stirred up between English and French Canadians during World War I. For the sake of national unity, he was determined not to repeat the mistakes of the past. The war as it unfolded, however, forced him to change his views on conscription.

Shortly after the evacuation at Dunkirk in June 1940, France surrendered to Nazi Germany. Britain might be invaded next. What if the British and French fleets fell into the hands of the Nazis? The east coast of Canada would then be vulnerable to attack and invasion.

This crisis led to the passing of the National Resources Mobilization Act (NRMA) in 1940, which required all men over 18 to register with the government for compulsory military service for the country's defence. The Act did not, however, give the government the power to send these conscripts to fight overseas.

The Conscription Referendum

In a speech to Parliament on September 8, 1939, Mackenzie King had said: "The present government believes that conscription of men for overseas service will not be a necessary or effective step." By 1942, King faced pressure from the Armed Forces and English Canada to authorize overseas conscription. A referendum in April 1942 seemed the best answer to his dilemma. Would the Canadian people release King from his promise never to introduce conscription?

The wording of the referendum question was not perfectly clear: "Are you in favour of releasing the government from any obligations arising out of any past commitments restricting the methods of raising men for military service?"

Despite the fuzzy wording, the results were clear as crystal. In Ontario 82.3% of voters marked their ballots "Yes." In British Columbia 79.4% voted in favour of overseas conscription. In Quebec, however, 72.9% of voters said "Non." King, who had pledged to preserve national unity, found he was caught squarely between the wishes of French and English voters, in the exact same position Robert Borden had found himself during World War I.

Figure 23-5 A family campaigns on behalf of conscription before the referendum in April 1942. Nationwide, 63% of Canadian voters voted "Yes" in the referendum, despite an overwhelming "No" vote in Quebec. By March 1944 an Armed Forces survey indicated that only 14% of its officers and 19% of its enlisted men could speak French.

Figure 23-6 The Conscription Crisis peaked in November 1944, when Mackenzie King was pressured into sending conscripts overseas. His Liberal government needed the help of the Cooperative Commonwealth Federation and the Social Credit Party to win a confidence vote in the House of Commons on December 7, 1944.

King decided he would not impose conscription for the time being. His policy would baffle people for years: "Not necessarily conscription, but conscription if necessary." What "necessary" meant was never explained.

The "Zombies" Go to War

By 1943, Canadian forces were fighting desperate battles in Italy, and on D-Day, June 6, 1944, they pushed into France. Casualties were high. The Armed Forces needed more men, and were willing to take even the reluctant soldiers drafted under the NRMA. These soldiers were called Zombies after creatures in a 1940s horror movie who lacked their own will and emotions.

By October 1944, Colonel James Ralston, Minister of National Defence, felt that the only solution to the Armed Forces' need for more soldiers was to send 16 000 Zombies to fight in Europe. Mackenzie King disagreed and forced Ralston to resign, replacing him with the popular general Andrew McNaughton, who promised he could raise more volunteers. In fact, he could not. By the end of November 1944, only 549 men had volunteered for overseas service. McNaughton then made the same recommendation that had cost Ralston his job: Send the Zombies abroad.

King gave in. The conscripts had to go, all 16 000 of them. Although a few deserted, most of the men accepted their fate. By the end of the war, 69 had been killed in combat, 232 wounded, and 13 were briefly taken prisoner by the Germans. The rapid collapse of Nazi Germany in 1945 relieved Canada of the need to send more conscripts to the front.

CROSSFIRE

THE ZOMBIES

The general... complaint is why people like these be allowed to live in this country and derive benefits from the efforts of Canadians, who are helping to win the war so that this country may remain free. When the peace has been won this will be a great country, and why should these spineless jellyfish be allowed to progress with the country when they have not had the courage to help her in times of trouble?

—A Canadian staff officer, quoted in W.A.B. Douglas and B. Greenhous, *Out of the Shadows* (Toronto: Oxford University Press, 1977), p. 245.

Some [Zombies] were idealistic young pacifists of the kind who had recently been signing pledges and taking part in freshman or high school debates against the whole idea of war. Others were French Canadians whose whole instinct and training told them to avoid the far-off, perpetual bloodshed of Europe... Many of them were, of course, and not unnaturally, scared stiff of the whole idea of being shot at. Some—and perhaps more of them than has yet been realized—would have been willing to fight anywhere their country told them to if others like them had been told the same.

—Ralph Allen, *Ordeal by Fire* (New York: Doubleday, 1961), p. 394.

RECONNECT

1. Explain how World War II affected the lives of Canadians on the homefront.

2. Why was Prime Minister Mackenzie King obliged to change his mind on the conscription issue?

FOCUS

This section will help you understand
  a. the contributions that women made to Canada's war effort at home
  b. the kinds of work that women members of the Armed Forces did.

Women in the Labour Force

Women played a very important role in Canada's war effort. By late 1944, more than one million women were working full time in Canada's labour force. A further 800 000 did farm work, often without pay. More than 250 000 women were employed in war production, making guns, ammunition, tanks, ships, and aircraft. There were women welders, drillers, electricians, and crane drivers, all quietly shattering the **stereotype** of women as homemakers.

War work paid well. A woman in the aircraft industry made about 83 cents an hour, compared with about 45 cents in the clothing industry. Women left low-paying jobs in droves to earn more money in war plants. Yet even in war industries, women still made only two-thirds of the wages of men doing identical jobs. This was a sore point, especially with women who were their family's sole support.

Volunteers

Women made one of their biggest contributions to the war effort through their traditional roles as homemakers and volunteer workers. It was Canada's homemakers who had to cope with shortages and rationing. They donated their time and skills to agencies like the Red Cross and worked in Armed Forces **canteens**. They grew Victory Gardens, canned fruits and vegetables, and performed a vast range of unglamorous but essential activities. The women who worked behind the scenes were the unsung, unpaid heroines of the war.

Women in Uniform

World War II was responsible for lowering one long-standing barrier for women: for the first time women were recruited into the Armed Forces. By war's end almost 50 000 women had enlisted: 20 497 in the CWAC (Canadian Women's Army Corps), 16 221 in the WDs (the Women's Division

Figure 24-1 These two women were among the more than quarter of a million who worked in the Canadian munitions industry during World War II.

Figure 24-2 The Canadian Army Women's Corps (CWAC), seen here recruiting in Manitoba, enrolled almost 21 000 women across the country. The poster behind the recruiters notes that for each woman who signed up, one more man would be released for active service.

of the RCAF), and 6665 in the WRENS (Women's Royal Canadian Naval Service). An additional 4439 served as Nursing Sisters in the three forces.

Many of these women served overseas, about 3800 in Britain alone.

The main function of women in the Armed Forces was to free men from desk jobs for combat duty. The great majority of servicewomen were employed as stenographers, clerks, and cooks. They were not considered suitable for combat duty, despite the fact that thousands of Russian women were combat troops and thousands of women in Nazi-occupied Europe fought and died in partisan and resistance movements.

Women's Liberation?

Social attitudes are slow to change. It would be unrealistic to think that six years of wartime service would radically change the status of women in Canada. Canadian women were not "liberated" as a result of their efforts during the war. Many working women bitterly resented the attitude that developed towards them as the war drew to a close. They were expected to gladly surrender the jobs they had been working at for years to their husbands and brothers who were returning to the workforce.

Figure 24-3
This uncaptioned cartoon appeared in the September 15, 1945 issue of Maclean's. See if you can write an appropriate caption for it in the form of dialogue between the two characters.

Drawn for Maclean's by Vic Herman

In 1946 all three women's military services were disbanded. The percentage of full-time women employees in Canada fell from a high of 33.5% in 1944, to a low of 23.6 % in 1954. Not until 1966 would women's employment figures climb back to the wartime high. The seeds of social change, however, had been sown.

EyeWitness

"Women Fought a War"

Husbands and boyfriends came back from the war and found their wives and girlfriends just weren't prepared to start washing dishes again. It must have been quite a shock. But some women had ferried air force bombers to Britain, and others drove ambulances and worked in canteens serving the troops, or in war plants handling very expensive tools, working on equipment, planes, instrument panels, and things, and the companies found they could do better than men. It is no lie… And also, and don't you forget this, she found she enjoyed working outside, with real live people and not being cooped up in a home and talking baby-talk to an 18-month-old and a three-year-old.

You could almost say that women fought a war the same as their men, the war against them just being women, household machines.

—*Woman war worker, quoted in Barry Broadfoot,* Six War Years.

RECONNECT

1. What evidence is there to suggest that women did not achieve social equality despite their great contributions during World War II?

2. How did women prove during the war that they were much more than homemakers?

FOCUS

This section will help you understand
  a. why the United States entered World War II
  b. why Canada began the drift to the U.S. sphere of influence and away from Great Britain.

TIMELINE — December 7, 1941

Dawn — The sun rises over Pearl Harbor on a sleepy Sunday morning. The American ships on Battleship Row lie quietly at berth, their crews suspecting nothing.

6:00 a.m. — The first wave of 183 Japanese torpedo-bombers and fighters leave their aircraft carriers.

7:02 a.m. — Two radar operators at Pearl Harbor see unknown aircraft on their screen. They assume the incoming aircraft are American airplanes scheduled to arrive from California. They close the station down shortly afterwards.

7:55 a.m. — The first Japanese attack, which lasts about 30 minutes, sends dive-bombers against the vessels on Battleship Row. Within seconds, chaos reigns as the Sunday-morning calm is shattered by a barrage of explosions and alarms: the deafening blast when torpedoes find their targets, the insistent blaring of ships' horns; loudspeakers announcing the all-too-obvious message—"Air raid! No drill!"

8:40 a.m. — The second wave of 180 Japanese airplanes continues the destruction with a series of high-level bombing runs.

9:45 a.m. — The Japanese aircraft withdraw, their pilots victorious.

The Aftermath of Pearl Harbor

The success of the Japanese attack on Pearl Harbor was shocking. They damaged or destroyed 18 warships and 188 aircraft. They killed 2333 U.S. service personnel and wounded 1347. By contrast, the Japanese lost only 29 aircraft.

The Japanese victory neutralized the U. S. Pacific Fleet for more than a year. On closer analysis, however, the victory was incomplete. The primary targets of the raid, three aircraft carriers, were on manoeuvres in the Pacific and escaped destruction. Most of the ships that were sunk or damaged were later restored to fighting trim. Also, the Japanese

Figure 25-1 Smoke pours from the USS West Virginia during the Pearl Harbor attack. In the background is the USS Tennessee. Moored side-by-side, the seven ships in "Battleship Row" made easy targets for the Japanese torpedo planes in the first wave of the attack.

made a serious mistake when they decided to cancel a third wave of bombers and head for home. If they had destroyed the American fuel supplies and the repair and docking facilities at Pearl Harbor, the United States would have taken much longer to recover.

Politically, the Japanese had blundered badly. Their "day of infamy," as U. S. President Franklin Roosevelt called it, united the American people behind a total war effort in the drive to defeat Japan. The Japanese had chosen to go to war with a military and industrial giant.

Hitler also blundered by supporting his Axis ally and declaring war on the United States immediately after Pearl Harbor. By doing this, he handed Britain and Russia the most powerful nation on earth as an ally.

Drawing Together: Canadian-American Cooperation

Before being plunged into the war by Pearl Harbor, the U.S. had sought ways of supporting the Allied cause while still maintaining its **neutrality**. In August 1940, after a series of Nazi military successes in Western Europe, President Roosevelt invited Prime Minister Mackenzie King to Ogdensburg, New York to discuss common concerns over the defence of North America.

The two leaders signed the Ogdensburg Agreement, which announced the creation of a Permanent Joint Board of Defence to study "land, sea, and air problems" and the "defence of the Northern half of the Western Hemisphere." Mackenzie King was very pleased with the Agreement, and he had visions of playing the role of a dealmaker in future negotiations between the U.S. and Britain.

By 1941, both Britain and Canada were having difficulty financing the war. Mackenzie King's

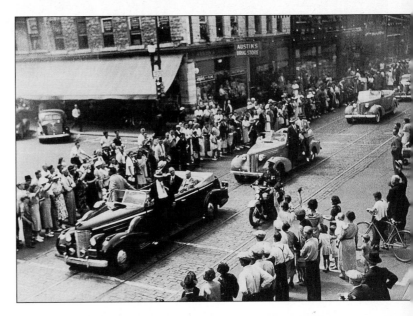

Figure 25-2 U.S. President Franklin Roosevelt waves to the crowds on Princess Street in Kingston in 1938. Beside him is Prime Minister Mackenzie King. In a speech at Queen's University, Roosevelt pledged that the U. S. "will not stand idly by" if Canada is "threatened by any other empire."

dreams of playing a pivotal diplomatic role were realized with the signing of the Hyde Park Declaration in April 1941, which established the **Lend-Lease** program. The warm relationship that had developed between Mackenzie King and Roosevelt greatly eased the negotiations leading up to the signing of the Declaration. The Lend-Lease program meant the U.S. could loan war materials to Great Britain and Canada without becoming directly involved in the war. (The attack on Pearl Harbor was still eight months away.) In return for its loans, the U. S. gained access to British-owned military bases.

By drawing closer to the United States, Canada was once again asserting its independence from Great Britain.

RECONNECT

1. What were the major results of the Japanese attack on Pearl Harbor?

2. Why was close cooperation with the United States so important to Canada and Britain during the early years of the war?

FOCUS

This section will help you understand
a. that Japanese Canadians were forcibly evacuated from British Columbia during World War II
b. the hardships that Japanese Canadians suffered as a result of this evacuation.

Japan attacked Pearl Harbor on December 7, 1941 and captured Hong Kong from its British and Canadian defenders on December 25. These events, coming so hard upon each other, set in motion a wave of anti-Japanese hysteria in British Columbia, where 22 000 Japanese Canadians lived, mostly in small coastal villages. About 14 000 of these people were **Nisei**, born and raised in Canada.

Many British Columbians were afraid that Japanese Canadians would commit acts of spying and sabotage. They thought those who owned fishing boats might use their short-wave radios to direct Japanese submarine and air attacks against coastal targets. Politicians in Victoria and Ottawa, even though they were aware there was no evidence of such acts of hostility against Canada, were quick to respond to public prejudice and pressure.

On January 14, 1942, for "reasons of national security," the federal cabinet forbade Japanese Canadians from fishing for the duration of the war. About 1200 of their boats were impounded and later sold at auction for rock-bottom prices. Japanese Canadians were not allowed to operate short-wave radios or cameras, and their purchases of gasoline were severely restricted. The government also ordered the evacuation of all Japanese Canadian males between the ages of 18 and 45.

On February 24, 1942, under the authority of the War Measures Act, the federal government passed an order-in-council that gave the B.C. Security Commission the power to remove all Japanese Canadians from a 100-mile-wide "protected zone" along the B.C. coast.

More than 20 000 Japanese Canadians were evacuated. About half were sent to live in hastily built detention camps in places like Slocan and Tashme in the interior of British Columbia. Men over 18 were forced to work in road camps, women and children were sent to live elsewhere. Families who didn't want to be split up were shipped to Alberta and Manitoba to work on sugar-beet farms. The government auctioned off everything these people left behind, including their homes and businesses.

Repatriation

On August 4, 1944, Prime Minister Mackenzie King said in the House of Commons: "It is a fact that no person of Japanese race born in Canada has been charged with any act of sabotage or disloyalty during the war." That was the "good" news. The bad news was that on December 15, 1945, three months after the end of the war, the federal cabinet passed orders-in-council that gave all Japanese Canadians the choice of "voluntary **repatriation**" to war-torn Japan or resettlement "east of the Rockies."

The government stated that it would consider those who chose to stay in B.C. "disloyal." In the end, 4000 went to Japan, before the Canadian public put pressure on the government to stop deporting its own citizens. On January 24, 1947, the orders-in-council were revoked, despite vehement objections from B.C. MPs. The Japanese Canadians who did move to Japan pined for their homes in Canada. Over the next 15 years or so, hundreds would return.

Figure 26-1
This photo from 1941 shows a fleet of impounded fishing boats that had belonged to Japanese Canadians.

CultureLink

Japanese Canadian poet and novelist Joy Kogawa was six years old when she was interned with her family in 1942. She spent most of the next three years in the internment camp at Slocan City.

WHAT DO I REMEMBER OF THE EVACUATION?

What do I remember of the evacuation?
I remember my father telling Tim and me
About the mountains and the train
And the excitement of going on a trip.
What do I remember of the evacuation?
I remember my mother wrapping
A blanket around me and my
Pretending to fall asleep so she would be happy
Though I was so excited I couldn't sleep
(I hear there were people herded
Into the Hastings Park like cattle.
Families were made to move in two hours
Abandoning everything, leaving pets
And possessions at gun point.
I hear families were broken up
Men were forced to work. I heard
It whispered late at night
That there was suffering) and
I missed my dolls.

What do I remember of the evacuation?
I remember Miss Foster and Miss Tucker
Who still live in Vancouver
And who did what they could
And loved the children and who gave me
A puzzle to play with on the train.
And I remember the mountains and I was
Six years old and I swear I saw a giant
Gulliver of Gulliver's Travels scanning the horizon
And when I told my mother she believed it too
And I remember how careful my parents were
Not to bruise us with bitterness
And I remember the puzzle of Lorraine Life
Who said "Don't insult me" when I
Proudly wrote my name in Japanese
And Tim flew the Union Jack
When the war was over but Lorraine
And her friends spat on us anyway
And I prayed to the God who loves
All the children in his sight
That I might be white.

—Joy Kogawa, A Choice of Dreams *(Toronto: McClelland & Stewart, 1974), pp. 54-55.*

CONNECTIONS

THE REDRESS SETTLEMENT

After years of political pressure, the government of Canada signed a Redress Agreement on August 26, 1988 with the National Association of Japanese Canadians (NAJC). The agreement included the following terms:

• an acknowledgement that the treatment of Japanese Canadians during and after World War II was unjust and violated principles of human rights;

• a tax-free lump sum payment of $21 000 to each surviving Japanese Canadian who had been subjected to internment, relocation, or deportation; and

• an arrangement whereby the NAJC contributed $12 million to a national foundation for the elimination of racism and the government of Canada matched that amount.

Figure 26-2
Canadian-born Yukiko and Sakon (Don) Sato at the Slocan City train station in 1946, getting ready to leave Canada for Japan. Both stayed in Japan until 1960, when they returned to Canada.

RECONNECT

1. Why did the Canadian government feel justified in:
   a. forcibly interning Japanese Canadians during the war?
   b. repatriating them to Japan after the war was over?

2. What evidence is there that the government's action against Japanese Canadians was wrong?

FOCUS

This section will help you understand
   a. that Canada waged a secret war of **espionage** whose importance rivalled that of the war on the battlefield
   b. the misery suffered by Canadian prisoners of war.

Canada's Secret War

One of the best-kept secrets of World War II was the existence of Camp X on the north shore of Lake Ontario, between Whitby and Oshawa. In its two years of existence, the camp produced 500 graduates, half of whom became spies, secret agents, and guerrilla fighters. Their task, according to British Prime Minister Winston Churchill, was to "set Europe ablaze."

Training at Camp X was very tough. You had to be able to parachute jump by night, use high explosives, communicate in code, organize and inspire civilian resistance groups, and, if captured, resist torture.

Two Canadian Secret Agents

GUSTAVE BIELER

Gustave Bieler was the first Canadian Special Operations Executive (SOE) agent to work in occupied France. After four months of training, Bieler parachuted into France. He was captured with his radio operator in January 1944.

Months of torture by the Gestapo failed to break Bieler, and this won him the respect of his captors. When Bieler was marched to his death in September 1944, he was granted the unusual "privilege" of being shot by a firing squad instead of hanged.

HENRY FUNG

Henry Fung was the first Chinese-Canadian agent to be parachuted into Malaya, in June 1945. Only 19 years old, he worked with an SOE team, blowing up telephone lines and railway bridges, and harassing Japanese road convoys. When he fell ill with malaria and jaundice, Henry was evacuated to Britain and eventually made his way home to Canada.

Henry Fung was one of hundreds of young Chinese-Canadians who volunteered for SOE service.

The Enigma and Ultra Decoders

In 1939, Polish agents managed to escape to Britain with the secret of the German coding machine. This device was called "Enigma," which comes from a Greek word meaning "mystery." The Germans believed that the Enigma code was unbreakable.

Armed with the Enigma secret, the British spy service was able to assemble another machine, called "Ultra," to unscramble German coded messages. From the very beginning of the war, British agents (and later, the Americans) were able to obtain vital information about the military activities of Nazi Germany. The knowledge that the German codes had been broken was one of the best-kept secrets of the war.

CaseStudy

CHURCHILL'S DILEMMA

Did Winston Churchill know, thanks to the Ultra decoder, that the English city of Coventry would be bombed on the night of November 14, 1940? World War II Canadian spymaster William Stephenson thought Churchill deliberately refused to warn the citizens of Coventry about the impending attack.

> If the Prime Minister evacuated Coventry, as he so desperately wished to do, he would tell the enemy that he knew their plans. The value of... all that Ultra implied for the future would be lost. If the citizens were not warned, thousands might die or suffer. Churchill did not warn them, beyond the customary alerting of firefighting and ambulance services... The Germans struck on schedule: November 14. The raid was so devastating that Berlin boasted that every town in England would be "Coventryized."

—*William Stevenson*, A Man Called Intrepid *(New York: Harcourt Brace Jovanovich, 1974), p. 153.*

Figure 27-1 The Enigma machine was actually a keyboard scrambler that both coded and decoded top-secret messages.

Prisoners of War (POWs)
The Hong Kong Garrison

The Hong Kong garrison was a mixed force of about 14 000 British, Indian, Canadian, and Chinese soldiers. Defence equipment consisted of a few anti-aircraft guns, six airplanes, and a few small gunboats.

Two battalions of Canadian soldiers, the Winnipeg Grenadiers and the Royal Rifles from Quebec, totalling 1975 men, arrived in Hong Kong on November 16, 1941, under the command of Brigadier J. K. Lawson.

Less than a month later, on December 7, 1941, the Japanese attacked Hong Kong from the landward side. The defenders resisted bravely but were forced to surrender on Christmas day. Allied losses were 2445 killed, wounded, and missing. Canadian losses were 267 killed, including Brigadier Lawson, and 290 more were to die during 44 months of often brutal captivity.

Figure 27-2 The photo on the top shows Canadian troops arriving in Hong Kong in November 1941. The photo on the bottom shows these same troops when they were liberated from a Japanese POW camp in 1945. Canadian prisoners suffered from a number of tropical diseases in the camps, including pellagra and diphtheria. Disease was brought on by unsanitary conditions and the lack of a nutritious diet.

EyeWitness

Conditions in POW Camps

Canadian POWs were first interned on Hong Kong Island and on mainland China. Between January 1943 and April 1944, more than 1100 Canadians were moved to Japan to work as forced labourers, mainly in coal and iron ore mines. One survivor tells his story:

"One of my boys caught a rat and cooked it, and he saved me a small portion. I sat it on top of my rice while it was still hot, so I could taste that flavour through the rice. When you're starving, anything tastes good."

—CSM Red Windsor, POW, Japan

Source: Daniel Dancocks, In Enemy Hands: Canadian Prisoners of War, 1939-1945 *(Edmonton: Hurtig, 1983).*

RECONNECT

1. How did Canada participate in the "Secret War?"
2. Why was the battle of Hong Kong such a tragedy for Canadian forces?

FOCUS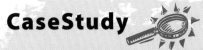

This section will help you understand

a. the role that Canadian troops played on D-Day and in the final liberation of Europe.

CaseStudy

D-DAY: OPERATION OVERLORD

The Allied invasion of Europe was code-named Operation Overlord. It was a complex and risky operation that called for careful coordination of air, naval, and land forces from Canada, Britain, and the United States.

PHASE I, AIR: BOMBING AND PARACHUTING

Aircraft would bomb and strafe German defences. They would also drop paratroopers and glider-borne shock troops to seize vital roads and bridges, and they would attempt to secure absolute control of the skies over Normandy.

PHASE II, NAVAL: CLEARING AND DELIVERING

Operation Neptune involved an armada of more than 7000 ships that had to clear lanes through minefields and bombard German positions. It was also up to the convoy to deliver more than 100 000 assault troops to the Normandy beaches, 20 000 vehicles, and a vast array of equipment, all to the right beach at the right time.

PHASE III, LAND FORCES: ASSAULTING AND SECURING

The First U.S. Army was assigned Utah and Omaha beaches, the Second British Army was to hit Gold and Sword beaches, and Canadian forces were to assault Juno Beach. The main objective of all forces was to secure a position in France from which further offensives could be launched.

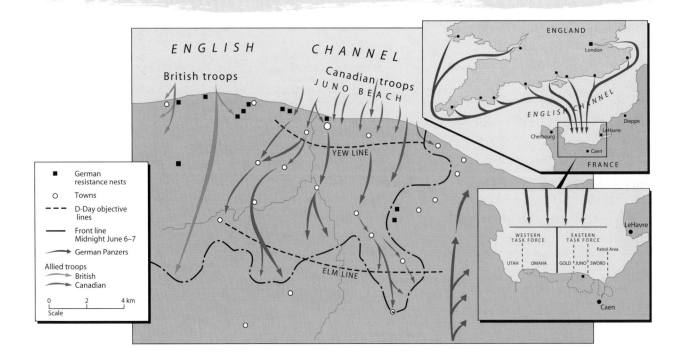

Figure 28-1 The first landing craft of Canada's Queen's Own Rifles hit Juno Beach at 8:12 a.m. on June 6, 1944. Canadian soldiers encountered booby-trapped beach obstacles and heavy fire from German machine-gun emplacements. Nevertheless, by nightfall some 14 000 Canadians had waded ashore and penetrated to within five miles of Caen, the furthest advance by any Allied division.

Canadian War Diary: From Normandy to Victory in Europe

Closing the Falaise Gap

July 29–August 21, 1944 In full retreat, the German army tries desperately to keep an escape route open through the French town of Falaise, between the advancing Canadian and American armies. Allied air planes strafe the Germans mercilessly as they try to move by daylight on the few roads still open to them. Germany's Seventh Army and Fifth Panzer Army are cut to pieces and 50 000 prisoners taken. On August 21, the Allies occupy Falaise, and all of Normandy is theirs.

Battle of the Scheldt

October 7–November 8, 1944 Opening the large Belgian port of Antwerp is essential to relieve Allied supply problems. First the estuary of the river Scheldt, between Antwerp and the sea, has to be cleared of Germans. This task is given to the First Canadian Army.

The Scheldt estuary is dead-flat country, reclaimed from the sea and divided by dikes. British bombers blast through the dikes and flood the central part of

Figure 28-2 Canadian troops used amphibious vehicles called "Buffaloes" in their assault on the Scheldt estuary after British bombers destroyed the system of dikes that had kept the area dry.

an island so that amphibious vehicles can be used in the attack. After a bitter struggle, the German defenders give up on November 8. The Battle of the Scheldt costs the Canadians 6367 casualties but earns them lavish praise from the British for their achievement.

The End of the War

February—May, 1945 The Canadians spend much of the winter in trenches, getting an unpleasant taste of the kind of war their fathers fought in World War I. In early February, the Canadians take part in the Allied spring offensive. The Germans are caught in a two-front vise. The Western Allies begin to cross the Rhine on March 23 and drive deep into German territory. The Soviet Red Army, six million strong, squeezes the Germans inexorably from the East. On April 30, Adolf Hitler commits suicide, and by May 2, after vicious street-fighting, the Soviets eliminate all German resistance in Berlin.

On May 7, 1945, the German forces formally surrender. For the Canadian and other Allied troops in Europe the war is over. May 8 becomes known as VE-Day, Victory-in-Europe Day, and a focus for riotous celebrations. The Allies can now turn their attention to ending the war with Japan.

EyeWitness

The Halifax Riot

In Halifax , the VE-Day celebrations degenerated into a riot in which two people were killed.

On VE-Day, May 8, 1945, Halifax was closed down… There were some 7000 soldiers and 1700 sailors in the area, most of whom felt they had been victimized and abused by local establishments and had grown to hate the city. When the servicemen mingled with civilians on the streets, a jovial street party turned into a destructive rampage. Liquor stores were broken open… vandalism followed, with 564 business firms suffering damage to their premises (mostly broken windows but some arson) and 207 shops actually looted.

—*W. A. B. Douglas and B. Greenhous,* Out of the Shadows: Canada in the Second World War.

RECONNECT 💡

1. What role did Canadian forces play in the defeat of Germany?

2. Why was there a riot in Halifax on VE-Day?

FOCUS

This section will help you understand
   a.   the **Holocaust** was an attempt by the Nazis to kill all Jews in occupied Europe
   b.   that few Jewish refugees were admitted to Canada.

The Einsatzgruppen

Hitler launched "Operation Barbarossa," the invasion of the Soviet Union, on June 22, 1941. A special action squad, the Einsatzgruppen, followed in the wake of the regular German army, the Wehrmacht. This 3000-member squad, created by Reinhard Heydrich, Germany's Chief of Security Police, had a deadly mission. They were to hunt down and kill all Jews and Communist Party officials in the occupied Soviet Union.

By the end of the war they had executed some 1.5 million Jews by machine-gun and in specially adapted vans in which people were poisoned by carbon monoxide fumes. Yet, despite their grisly efficiency, the Einsatzgruppen did not kill Jews fast enough to satisfy their Nazi masters.

The Final Solution

Hitler had long blamed German Jews for the country's problems following World War I. After the invasion of Poland in 1939, he tried to carry out what he called the final solution, the mass murder of all European Jews. Trains from all over occupied Europe carried people to extermination camps such as Auschwitz, Treblinka, and Sobibor. There they were systematically starved or worked to death,

Primary Source
THE WANSEE CONFERENCE

On January 20, 1942, Heydrich called together top civil servants and **SS** officials at Wansee, near Berlin. He announced his plan to coordinate methods to murder all of Europe's Jews.

> The final solution to the Jewish problem in Europe will be applied to about 11 million people… The Jews must be transferred to the East under close surveillance and there assigned to forced labour… It goes without saying that a great many of them will be naturally eliminated by physical deficiency. The remainder who survive this must be dealt with accordingly.

Thus the monstrous system of concentration camps and mass liquidation of innocent people was set in motion.

or suffocated in gas chambers, their corpses buried in mass graves or reduced to ashes in ovens. The gold in their teeth, the hair on their heads, and all their usable possessions were harvested for the Nazi war effort.

Men like Adolf Eichmann supervised the so-called final solution with morbid dedication. Up until the end of the war, even in the face of certain defeat for Germany, trains and cattle trucks continued to deliver Jews to the extermination camps.

Figure 29-1   Three of the architects of the Nazis' Final Solution. From the left, Reinhard Heydrich, chief of the Security Police; Adolf Eichmann, head of the Gestapo department dealing with Jewish affairs; and Rudolf Hoess, commandant of Auschwitz. Hoess is shown listening to testimony at the Nuremberg Trials, where German war criminals were tried after the war.

Figure 29-2 The photo shows a warehouse at Auschwitz. It is full of shoes and clothing confiscated from prisoners who were gassed on their arrival. The following quotation is taken from testimony given by Rudolf Hoess, commandant of Auschwitz, at the Nuremberg trials. "We had two SS doctors on duty at Auschwitz to examine the incoming transports of prisoners. These would be marched by one of the doctors, who would make spot decisions as they walked by. Those who were fit to work were sent into the camp. Others were sent immediately to the extermination plants. Children of tender years were invariably exterminated since by reason of their youth they were unable to work."

EyeWitness

Auschwitz

We got used to standing in line at 7 o'clock in the morning, at 12 noon, and again at 7 o'clock in the evening. We got used to sleeping without beds, to saluting every uniform, not to walk on the sidewalks and then again to walk on the sidewalks. We got used to undeserved slaps, blows, and executions. We got used to seeing people die in their own excrement, to seeing piled-up coffins full of corpses, to seeing the sick amidst dirt and filth and to seeing the helpless doctors. We got used to it that from time to time, one thousand unhappy souls would come here and that, from time to time, another thousand unhappy souls would go away.

—From the prose of 15-year-old Petr Fischl, who died in Auschwitz in 1944. [J. Glatstein et al., eds., *Anthology of Holocaust Literature* (New York: Atheneum, 1980), p. 138.]

StatScan   Canada Closes Its Doors to Jewish Immigrants

Between 1935 and 1945, Canada had the worst record in the Western world when it came to admitting Jewish refugees from Europe. In their book *None Is Too Many*, Canadian historians Irving Abella and Harold Troper charged that a number of powerful Canadians during this period were anti-Semitic and deliberately blocked the entry of Jews into the country even though they were aware of the persecutions in Europe. Two who exercised great influence in this regard were Prime Minister Mackenzie King and Director of Immigration F. C. Blair.

Jewish Immigration, 1933–1945

Country Accepting Jewish Immigrants	Number of Immigrants
United States	200 000
Palestine	125 000
United Kingdom	70 000
Argentina	50 000
Brazil	27 000
Australia	15 000
Canada	5 000

Source: Irving Abella and Harold Troper, None is Too Many *(Toronto: Lester & Orpen Dennys, 1983), p. vi.*

RECONNECT

1. How was the machinery of the Holocaust organized and operated?
2. Why might Canada have to share some of the guilt for the Holocaust tragedy?

FOCUS

This section will help you understand
   a.   how devastating the atomic bombs were that were dropped on the cities of Hiroshima and Nagasaki
   b.   the connection between the dropping of the bombs and the end of World War II.

The Manhattan Project

When was the dawn of the nuclear age? You might say that July 16, 1945 was a day that changed the world forever. It was then that Allied scientists working on the **Manhattan Project** exploded the first atomic bomb in the desert at Alamagordo, New Mexico.

A flash of nuclear fire leaped from ground zero, bathing the desert in a blinding white light. The steel tower from which the bomb was dropped vapourized in temperatures 10 000 times hotter than the surface of the sun. Within a radius of two kilometres of the explosion's **epicentre**, all animal life vanished. The nuclear age had arrived.

The Manhattan Project, which the U. S. government established in 1942, had important links to Canada. Several Canadian scientists worked on the project. Also, uranium, the most vital ingredient in the A-bomb, was mined in a high-grade form at Great Bear Lake in the Northwest Territories. Canada also had, at Port Hope, Ontario, the only uranium refinery outside Nazi Europe.

Figure 30-1 On July 26, 1945, U. S. President Harry Truman, Soviet Premier Josef Stalin, and Clement Atlee, the new British prime minister, issued the Potsdam Declaration to Japan. This was an ultimatum calling for unconditional surrender. Any

Hiroshima and Nagasaki

August 6, 1945 dawned a beautiful, clear day in southern Japan. At 8:15 a.m., three U. S. B-29 bombers approached Hiroshima, a port city of 350 000 on the southern coast of Honshu, Japan's main island. One of the planes, the "Enola Gay," dropped a four-ton bomb that detonated 300 metres above the city's centre.

There followed the greatest man-made explosion that had occurred up to that time. Between 70 000 and 100 000 people were incinerated in the terrible firestorm that swept through the city, destroying 60 000 buildings. Another 80 000 people were injured, some with horrifying burns.

People near the epicentre of the explosion were simply vapourized, leaving only their shadows burned into asphalt pavements and concrete walls. A huge mushroom cloud formed above Hiroshima, and a black radioactive rain fell, inflicting a lingering death on thousands.

Three days later the U. S. dropped a second A-bomb, nicknamed "Fat Man," on Nagasaki, killing an additional 40 000 people. At noon on August 15, Emperor Hirohito announced in a radio broadcast to his people that Japan would surrender unconditionally to the Allies.

Canadians and the Pacific War

In April 1945, one month before VE-Day, Mackenzie King announced that no Canadian soldiers would be ordered to fight in the Pacific theatre. Anyone who volunteered to fight against the Japanese would first be given 30 days' leave in Canada. There were about 80 000 volunteers, but the war against Japan was over before any of them saw combat.

delay would mean "the inevitable and complete destruction of the Japanese armed forces, and… the utter devastation of the Japanese homeland." When Japan did not reply, Truman set in motion the first use in history of a nuclear weapon.

Apart from the two battalions sent to Hong Kong and several RCAF squadrons that flew missions in Burma, Canada played little part in the war with Japan. Perhaps for this reason, the VJ-Day (Victory over Japan) celebrations on August 15 were subdued compared with the outpourings of relief and joy that marked VE-Day.

Figure 30-2 The ruins of Hiroshima after the dropping of the atomic bomb.

Figure 30-3 As chief representative of the Allied forces, U.S. General Douglas MacArthur accepted the Japanese surrender. Representatives of the nine Allied countries, including Canada, signed the document on September 2, 1945. After six years and one day of bitter fighting, World War II was over.

BIOGRAPHY

Subject: Louis Slotin

Dates: 1912–1946

Figure 30-4 Louis Slotin

Most Notable Accomplishment: Slotin was invited to work on the Manhattan Project at Los Alamos, New Mexico as the U.S. raced to beat Nazi Germany in the development of an atomic bomb.

Thumbnail Sketch: Louis Slotin was one of several brilliant Canadian scientists who worked on the Manhattan Project. Slotin became an object lesson in the dangers of handling radioactive materials. One of his experiments was the creation of **critical mass**. This involved joining uranium and plutonium to the point where the neutron count increased to a critical state. He would then separate them before an explosion occurred. Slotin called this risky procedure "tickling the dragon's tail."

On May 21, 1946, as Slotin was conducting a critical mass experiment, there was a slight maladjustment of the uranium and plutonium spheres. The neutron counter blew off the scale, and the laboratory was filled with a brilliant blue light.

Before an explosion could occur, Slotin separated the spheres with his bare hands, receiving a lethal dose of radiation. He died after nine days of agony.

RECONNECT

1. What were the major results of the dropping of the atomic bombs on Japan?

2. How did Canada participate in the development of the atomic bomb?

31 The United Nations

> **If the UN didn't exist, we'd have to invent it.**
> —*Stephen Lewis, former Canadian ambassador to the UN.*

TIMELINE 1945-1997

1945	World War II ends and the UN is formed.
1947	The Truman Doctrine and the Marshall plan are put into effect.
1948	The UN Declaration of Human Rights is signed.
	The Berlin Blockade and Airlift.
1949	NATO is formed.
1950	The Korean War begins (ending in 1953).
1955	Warsaw Pact is signed.
1956	The Suez Crisis.
1961	The Berlin Wall is built.
1962	The Cuban Missile Crisis.
1976	End of the Vietnam War.
1979	The Soviets invade Afghanistan.
1989	The Berlin Wall falls.
1991	A speech by Mikhail Gorbachev marks the end of the Cold War.
	Civil war begins in the former Yugoslavia.
1992	The Canadian Airborne Regiment goes to Somalia.
1997	The Somalia Inquiry submits its report, condemning the high command of the Canadian Armed Forces for "leadership failures."

In the spring of 1945, as World War II was ending, Canada and some 50 other nations met in San Francisco to form a world-wide organization. Its aim was to eliminate the kind of conflict that had resulted in two world wars in the first half of the century. The original UN charter was signed on June 26, 1945.

As we have seen, this was not the first time such an organization had been formed. The League of Nations had been set up in 1919, after World War I. It was supposed to resolve international disputes and so guarantee world security. In reality the League turned out to be powerless. This was largely because several of the most powerful countries in the world, including the United States, were not members.

After World War II, the need for a new organization was obvious. The war had caused an estimated $1.5 billion a day in damage, and killed about 35 million people. The leaders of Germany and Japan were put on trial for "crimes against humanity." This was the first time in history that the losing side was charged with atrocities committed during a war. The Germans had killed some nine million civilians, and the Japanese had mistreated and killed thousands of military and civilian prisoners of war.

THE PURPOSES OF THE UNITED NATIONS

- To maintain international peace and security.

- To develop friendly relations among nations.

- To cooperate internationally in solving economic, social, cultural, and humanitarian problems and in promoting respect for basic human rights.

THE UN IS DIVIDED INTO SIX PARTS

1. The General Assembly
- Each of the 185 member states has a seat.
- The Assembly meets every year from the third Tuesday in September until mid-December. Special meetings can be called if there is an international emergency.
- The Assembly can only *recommend* action on any issue. It cannot force a nation to do what it desires.

2. The Security Council
- The five permanent members are China, France, Russia, the United States, and the United Kingdom. Each has a **veto**.
- The General Assembly elects 10 non-permanent members to the Council for 2-year terms.
- The Council meets all year long. All members must be on call 24 hours a day.
- If there is a threat to peace, the council can order economic sanctions against the aggressor, and all members of the UN have to follow. If sanctions fail, the Council can take military action. This has happened only twice: Korea in 1950, and the Persian Gulf in 1990.
- Canada has sat on the Council for five separate 2-year terms.

3. The Economic and Social Council
- There are 54 member states elected for 3-year terms. Each member has one vote. To make a decision a simple majority (51%) is required.
- The council only meets once a year, but does over three-quarters of the UN's work.

4. The International Court of Justice
- There are 15 judges elected by the General Assembly and the Security Council.
- The Court hears cases brought to it by UN member states. No individual can bring cases before the Court.

5. The Secretariat
- This group provides administrative services that keep the UN running.
- About 25 000 people work in 163 Secretariat offices around the world. One-third of them work in New York.
- The Secretariat uses about 65% of the UN's budget and helps run some 2000 programs.

6. The Trusteeship Council
- The work of this council is virtually finished. There are no countries left that are under foreign administration. The structure of the UN will probably be reformed soon and the Council will be eliminated.

Figure 31-1 The Security Council. Each of the five permanent members of the Security Council can block actions recommended by all the other members. *All* members of the Security Council have used this veto power at least once.

Figure 31-2 In the General Assembly, the members sit in alphabetical order and each nation has one vote. The assembly operates in six languages: Arabic, Chinese, English, French, Russian, and Spanish. Simultaneous translation of all speeches into each of these languages is available.

The Declaration of Human Rights

The UN's Declaration of Human Rights was signed in 1948. It was drafted by a Canadian named John Humphrey, a law professor at McGill University. He later became the first director of the Division of Human Rights in the UN.

The document has 30 sections, but its message is contained in the introduction. Here it is in a simplified form:

▶ Human rights for all are the basis of freedom, justice, and peace.

▶ The denial of human rights has led to horrific events. A world where humans enjoy freedom of speech and belief, and freedom from fear, is the greatest goal.

▶ Human rights have to be protected by law.

▶ Friendly relations between nations must be promoted.

▶ The Charter of the UN emphasizes equal rights for men and women and promotes the idea of a better life with freedom for all.

▶ The members of the UN pledge to achieve respect for human rights and freedoms.

▶ To accomplish this pledge, there must be an understanding of what these rights and freedoms mean.

Figure 31-3 John Humphrey is shown in the late 1940s with his boss, Eleanor Roosevelt, who was then head of the UN's Human Rights Commission.

HUMAN RIGHTS ISSUES

Figure 31-5
Nelson
Mandela

Women's Rights World-wide, there are many examples of discrimination against women. In many places, women do not know their rights and are treated as virtual slaves. They tend to be given less education than men, do more work, and die younger. Figure 31–4 shows an Indian woman who sold one of her kidneys for badly needed cash.

Race Relations Racial injustice is also a common problem around the world. It was very much in evidence in South Africa when **apartheid** was still official government policy. Because he fought for equal rights for Blacks, Nelson Mandela was placed in prison for 27 years. With the help of many UN member nations, he was finally released in 1990 and became the president of his country.

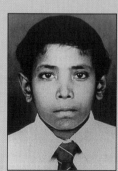

Figure 31-4

Political Disappearances A political disappearance is the seizure and hiding away of a person by a government. Usually the person is someone who disagrees with the government's policies. Their disappearance is often the first step to their torture and execution. Age is no barrier to a person suffering this type of repression. Gnanaguru Aravinthan was only 13 years old when he was seized by the army in Sri Lanka in 1985. According to an Amnesty International newsletter, the boy was still missing in 1989, and as of 1997 there had been no further word on his whereabouts.

Figure 31-6
Gnanaguru Aravinthan

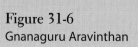

CaseStudy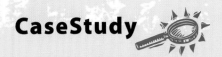

CRAIG KIELBURGER, CRUSADER AGAINST CHILD LABOUR

From the time he was 13 years old, Craig Kielburger, a resident of Thornhill, Ontario, has been waging an effective crusade against the exploitation of children in the workplace. In 1995, he founded an organization called Free the Children, which is committed to putting pressure on the leaders of the offending countries to stop child labour and make school compulsory. As part of his crusade, Craig has spoken to a number of world leaders, including Canadian Prime Minister Jean Chretien. He has recommended making child labour reforms a condition of signing any new trade deals. He has also lobbied for a ban against the importing products made by child labour.

Figure 31-7 Craig Kielburger at the age of 13. "There are children as young as five working chained to the ground in quarries, children in sugar cane fields, and children in dangerous glass factories."

Craig bases his work in part on Section 9 of the UN's Declaration of the Rights of the Child, which promises "Protection against all forms of neglect, cruelty, and exploitation."

UNICEF estimates that child labour affects about 200 million children world wide. Craig often cites figures from India, where there are 50 million child labourers (and about 55 million unemployed adults). Countries with large carpet-making industries are notorious for using child labourers, some of whom have to work 15 hours a day. Craig refers to the case of a young boy who tried to help his brother escape from the carpet makers and was branded with red-hot irons. Unfortunately many of these children are the sole supporters of their families and so are involved in a "no-win" situation.

N E T S U R F E R

ADDRESS: http://www.10.org/amnesty

DESCRIPTION: Originating from Amnesty International, this site contains general information, news releases, and the full text of appeal cases and documents dating from January 1994.

Founded in London in 1961, Amnesty International is dedicated to informing the public about human rights violations around the world. It focuses especially on abuses of free speech and freedom of religion. It also lobbies vigorously against the imprisonment and torture of political prisoners.

For its work in winning the release of political prisoners and prisoners of conscience, Amnesty International was awarded the 1977 Nobel Peace Prize. The logo of Amnesty International is a burning candle wrapped in barbed wire. What do you think this logo symbolizes?

RECONNECT

1. What are the central purposes of the UN?

2. In your view, what is the most important part of the UN? Why?

3. If you were choosing an issue within the human rights area for special attention, which would you choose and why?

FOCUS

This section will help you understand
  a. what was meant by the term "the Cold War"
  b. why the Cold War developed.

Taking Sides

Winning the war against Germany and Japan turned out to be easier for the Allies than keeping on good terms with each other once the war was over. As soon as World War II ended, the Cold War began. The two "superpowers," the United States and the Soviet Union, each had concerns that made them hostile to the other. The Soviets were worried about keeping their borders free from Western invasion. The U.S. and its allies were deeply concerned about the spread of communism. Soon much of the world was divided into two camps: the U.S. and its allies on one side, and the Soviet Union and the Eastern Bloc on the other.

The situation was called a "cold" war because no actual fighting ever developed between the two superpowers. Instead it was a war of propaganda, spying, and the use of military and economic aid to develop new allies and spheres of influence.

CaseStudy

THE ROLE OF THE U.S.

Figure 32-1
U.S. President Harry Truman and his Secretary of State George Marshall.

Like Canada, the United States was one of the few countries involved in World War II that did not suffer from invasion or devastating bombing campaigns. Thanks to its reserve of natural resources and its large population, the U.S. enjoyed a measure of wealth unequaled by any country in the world at the time.

Under President Harry Truman, the U.S. developed two policies that placed it in direct opposition to the Soviet Union.

The Truman Doctrine
The American "declaration of cold war" came on March 12, 1947, when the Truman Doctrine was announced. The main points were:
• a crusade against communism to stop its expansion,
• the announcement that the free peoples of the world could look to the U.S. to maintain their freedoms, and
• that the U.S. would give $400 million to the Greek and Turkish armies to stop the Soviets from expanding near their borders.

The Marshall Plan
Was all of Europe on the verge of turning to communism? Stalin thought so. Britain, France, and Italy were having problems recovering from the devastation of the war, and it looked as if communist governments might be elected in France and Italy.

U.S. leaders believed that to avoid a communist sweep of Europe, the people would have to experience a better standard of living. Secretary of State George Marshall developed the European Economic Recovery Program, which came to be known as the Marshall Plan. It offered financial aid to any European country that requested it to help in the post-war recovery. The Soviet-backed nations rejected the plan because it was American. Instead, they accepted aid from the Soviet Union under a program called the Molotov Plan.

Between 1948 and 1952, the Marshall Plan distributed $13.5 billion to 16 European countries. Canada contributed $1.6 billion of this in the form of exported goods.

The Iron Curtain

In 1946, two world leaders gave speeches that helped to define the Cold War. On February 9, the Soviet Union's leader, Josef Stalin, gave his "two worlds" speech. The world had been divided into two hostile camps, Stalin claimed, **communism** and **capitalism**. War between the two worlds was inevitable.

A month later, on March 5, Winston Churchill gave a speech at a college in Fulton, Missouri. "From Stettin in the Baltic to Trieste in the Adriatic," he said, "an iron curtain has descended across the continent... This is certainly not the liberated Europe we fought to build up."

The End of the Cold War

Over the years, there were several Cold War conflicts, including the Korean War, the War in Vietnam, the Cuban Missile Crisis, and the Soviet invasion of Afghanistan in 1979. In some of these the U.S. and the Soviet Union came perilously close to all-out war.

In 1985, Mikhail Gorbachev became the new leader of the Soviet Union. Gorbachev had studied law and crop production at Moscow University. In 1978, he was appointed to the influential position of Agricultural Secretary in the Soviet government. As General Secretary of the Communist Party, he immediately introduced some dramatic changes to Soviet society, including the policies of **glasnost** (openness) and **perestroika** (restructuring). In 1987, largely as a result of Gorbachev's efforts, the Soviet-American arms-control treaty was signed.

One of the greatest changes that Gorbachev made was the introduction of free elections in the Soviet Union. He also encouraged a free market system. For his efforts in ending the Cold War, Gorbachev received the Nobel Peace prize in 1990.

When he resigned as president of the Soviet Union on December 25, 1991, Gorbachev said, "We are now living in a new world. An end has been put to the Cold War."

Figure 32-2 The Cold War arrived in Canada very soon after World War II ended. On a September evening in 1945, Igor Gouzenko, a cipher clerk at the Soviet embassy in Ottawa, left the embassy with secret documents. The papers proved that the U.S.S.R. was operating a spy ring in Canada and the U.S. This was a great shock since only a month before the Soviets had been a wartime ally.

Figure 32-3 An editorial cartoon from Soviet Russia charging that the wealthy U.S. ignores its poor. The label on the poor man's back reads "Five million unemployed." Who does the small man in the tuxedo represent?

Figure 32-4 Mikhail Gorbachev.

RECONNECT

1. Explain in your own words why the Cold War developed between nations that had been allies during World War II.

2. How did Mikhail Gorbachev help to end the Cold War?

NATO

As the Cold War developed, there were several incidents that intensified the bad feelings between the West and the Soviet Union. In 1948 alone, the Soviets blockaded Berlin and sponsored a communist takeover of Czechoslovakia. Canada was one of the first Western nations to call for a defensive organization that would have *a flexible response* capability, that is, the ability to respond with whatever weapons seemed necessary. On April 4, 1949, the North Atlantic Treaty Organization (NATO) came into being.

Membership in NATO is expensive. After the Cold War ended, both Canada and the U.S. threatened to pull out. Instead of falling apart, however, NATO has continued to grow. This is partly in response to continuing turmoil in Europe, for example, in Bosnia and Herzegovina. In July 1997, the members of NATO voted to allow three former Warsaw Pact members to join the alliance: Hungary, Poland, and the Czech Republic.

The Warsaw Pact

The two World Wars took a higher toll in lives from the Soviet Union than from any other country involved. To protect itself from another disastrous war, the Soviet Union kept its forces in the Eastern European countries it occupied at the end of World War II. With this "buffer" in place, it would be more difficult to invade the U.S.S.R. from the west.

The Soviets looked on NATO as a threat, especially when their most hated enemy, West Germany, was allowed to join in 1955. In response, they created their own alliance, the Warsaw Pact, on May 14, 1955. Combined action by Warsaw Pact members put violent ends to independence movements in Hungary (1956) and in Czechoslovakia (1968). This alliance collapsed in 1991 after the end of the Cold War, and a number of the original members have applied to join NATO.

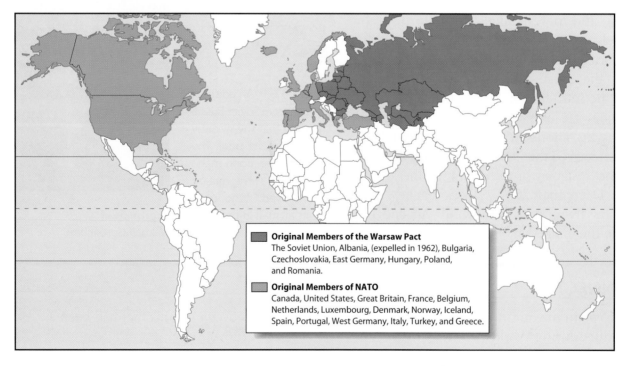

Original Members of the Warsaw Pact
The Soviet Union, Albania, (expelled in 1962), Bulgaria, Czechoslovakia, East Germany, Hungary, Poland, and Romania.

Original Members of NATO
Canada, United States, Great Britain, France, Belgium, Netherlands, Luxembourg, Denmark, Norway, Iceland, Spain, Portugal, West Germany, Italy, Turkey, and Greece.

Figure 33-2 In the years after World War II, most of the countries in Europe joined one of two major alliances, NATO for the Western nations, and the Warsaw Pact for those allied to the U.S.S.R.

NORAD

During World War II, North America had been safe from invasion and bombing attacks. By 1957, however, the Soviet Union had developed an impressive nuclear arsenal that included atomic and hydrogen bombs and bombers and missiles capable of delivering these bombs great distances. On May 12, 1958, Canada and the U.S. signed the North American Air Defence Command agreement (NORAD). The headquarters for NORAD are in Colorado. The commander-in-chief is always an American, and the second-in-command always a Canadian.

This agreement had three purposes:
▶ to monitor all missile launches around the world to see if they threatened North America.
▶ to operate radar systems that would warn of enemy aircraft or missiles headed for North America, and to intercept them.
▶ to monitor all satellites in outer space.

As time went on, NORAD became more and more concerned with the military threat posed by satellites, and in 1981 it changed its name to the North American Aerospace Defense Command (NAADC).

Nuclear Delivery Vehicles of the Powers, 1974					
	USA	**USSR**	**Britain**	**France**	**China**
Intercontinental ballistic missiles	1054	1575	–	–	–
Intermediate ballistic missiles	–	600	–	18	80
Submarine-based ballistic missiles	656	720	64	48	–
Long-range bombers	437	140	–	–	–
Medium-range bombers	66	800	50	52	100

Figure 33-2 One of the most alarming aspects of the two-alliance system was the arms race. Each side was determined to be stronger than the other. The result was that the U.S. and the Soviet Union competed to create the biggest stockpile of nuclear weapons. The realization that a nuclear war would be a disaster for both sides had little effect on reducing the stockpiles.

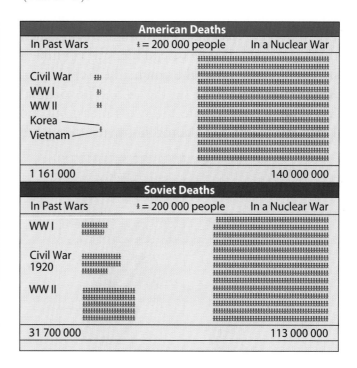

Figure 33-3 The number of casualties in the event of a nuclear war would be almost unimaginable. The U.S. would suffer the greatest losses.

C O N N E C T I O N S

In 1914, the existence of two defensive alliances, the Triple Entente and the Triple Alliance, helped to plunge Europe into World War I.

RECONNECT

1. The Cold War is over, so you might think that both alliances should disappear. NATO, however, is not only still in operation but growing. Why do you think this is so?

2. We have seen that in the past alliances have led to conflicts such as World War I. Do you think they can also help nations to avoid armed conflicts? Explain your answer.

FOCUS

This section will help you understand
a. how the United Nations got involved in the Korean War
b. the contributions Canadians made to the war.

The Cold War Heats Up

By the time World War II ended in 1945, Korea had been under Japanese control for 35 years. After the war, Korea was occupied by the Soviet Union and the United States. The country was divided in two at the 38th parallel. The northern half, called the Democratic People's Republic, was controlled by the Soviets, while the south, the Republic of Korea, was supported by the U.S. The original intention was to reunite the two Koreas, but the U.S.S.R and the U.S. could not agree about the best way of doing this. Each wanted to make sure that their own type of government was in control. As the Cold War worsened, the likelihood of an agreement grew less and less.

On June 25, 1950, an army from the People's Republic crossed the 38th parallel and invaded the south. On June 27, the United Nations called the Security Council into session and passed a resolution asking member states to provide military assistance to repel the invasion. The Soviets would certainly have vetoed this resolution, but through an incredible coincidence they were boycotting the Council at the time. So the resolution passed, and the Cold War turned into a very hot war. The Soviets made sure they never missed another meeting of the Security Council.

Canada's Participation

Canada was one of 14 countries that sent troops to Korea. Some 32 others also sent aid of various sorts. In addition to troops, Canada sent three destroyers and several aircraft to airlift supplies.

When the UN forces pushed the North Korean army back close to the Chinese border, thousands of Chinese soldiers poured over the border and helped beat the UN army back below the 38th parallel.

The first Canadian combat troops, the Princess Patricia's Light Infantry, arrived in Korea on December 18, 1950. They played a key role in the Battle of Kapyong, defending their position from repeated attacks over a three-day period. Their victory very likely prevented the capital of South Korea, Seoul, from falling into enemy hands and won the brigade a decoration from American president Harry Truman.

By the time a truce was called on July 27, 1953, the opposing forces were in almost the exact same positions they had started from in 1950.

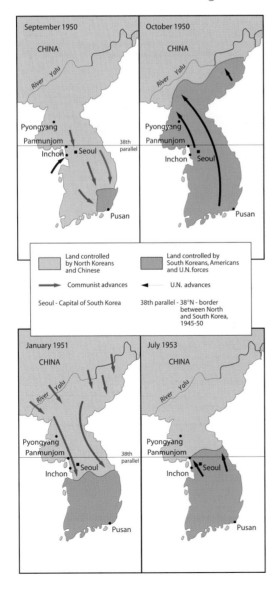

Figure 34-1 North and South Korea during the Korean War.

CultureLink
COMBAT POETRY

KOREA

There is blood on the hills of Korea,
'Tis blood of the brave and the true
Where the 25th Brigade battled together
Under the banner of the Red, White, and Blue.
As they marched over the fields of Korea
To the hills where the enemy lay,
They remembered the Brigadier's order:
These hills must be taken today.
Forward they marched into battle
With faces unsmiling and stern,
They knew as they charged the hillside
There were some who would never return…
There is blood on the hills of Korea,
It's the gift of the freedom they love;
May their names live in glory forever
And their souls rest in Heaven above.
—*Private Pat O'Connor, Stretcher bearer with the Royal Canadian Regiment, killed in action May 1951.*

Figure 34-2 Edward Zuber illustrated the confusion of battle in the Korean War with his painting titled "Contact."

Figure 34-3 Private Pat O'Connor.

EyeWitness

The Death of Pat O'Connor

About halfway up the peak, our No. 12 Platoon on the west ridge approached a small plateau on the upward path. Just as the first section moved through this small grove, we were startled by a burst of machine-gun fire from the edge of the path just ahead. Two or three bursts brought down most of this forward group and the move ahead was halted. All around the wounded were groaning and calling for help, while a corporal quietly died beside me.

Reaction was swift as a few of the rifles and sten guns commenced firing in the general direction of the machine-gun, and grenades were lobbed past the tiny plateau. Sporadic machine-gun bursts continued and there was much confusion as the fog of battle increased.

Suddenly I looked around and was surprised to see a soldier with a long stretcher over his shoulders come galloping up the path from below. Some of the boys in the rear sections had been calling for a "medic" and Paddy O'Connor, a company stretcher bearer, insisted on responding, although he had apparently been advised of the continuing danger. Just as he reached the spot where I was crouching, there was another burst of fire, and Paddy stumbled over his stretcher and rolled over dead.

Source: Don Stickland, quoted in John Gardam, Korea Volunteer: Oral History of Those There *(Burnstown, Ont.: General Store Publishing, 1994), pp. vi-vii.*

RECONNECT

1. Why was Korea divided after World War II?

2. Why did the UN send troops to Korea?

3. In your view, should Canadian troops have fought in Korea?

FOCUS

This section will help you understand
a. how the Suez Crisis developed
b. what role Canada played in establishing the UN's "peacekeeping" force.

War in the Middle East

On October 29, 1956, Israel attacked Egypt and occupied the Sinai Desert. Why did this happen? In 1954 an Egyptian army colonel, Gamal Nasser, overthrew the government. By 1956 he had become president of a country that was poor and relatively undeveloped. The British and the Americans had both promised Nasser financial aid to build the Aswan Dam on the Nile River.

This dam would help Egypt become economically self-sufficient by providing electricity and irrigation water. At the same time, Nasser meant to buy military equipment from Czechoslovakia, which was in the **Soviet Bloc**. For this reason Britain and the U.S. withdrew their offers of economic aid in July 1956. Pressed for money, Nasser seized control of the Suez Canal later that same month and

nationalized it. The Canal had been owned jointly by Britain and France. Nasser thought that the revenue from ships using the Canal could be used to help modernize Egypt and improve the people's standard of living. In the meantime, the Soviet Union had promised to give Nasser the funds necessary to build the Aswan Dam.

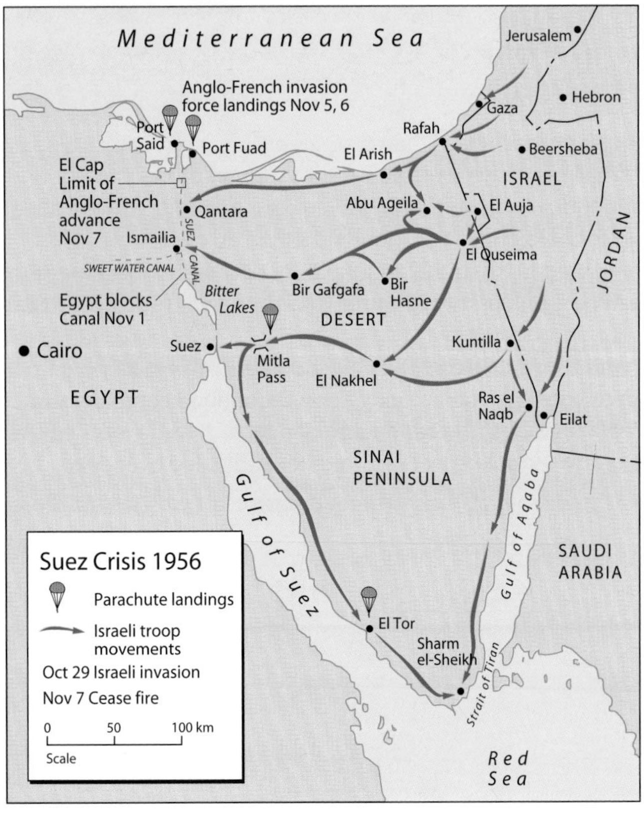

With Britain and France being pushed out of Egypt and the Soviet Union invited in, Israel felt it was now completely surrounded by hostile forces.

When Egypt blockaded the Israeli port city of Eilat, Israel struck back. Britain and France dropped paratroopers into the zone around the Suez Canal, claiming this was necessary to keep the Canal open to shipping. Both the U.S. and the Soviet Union voiced strong disapproval of Britain and France. It seemed for a time that all-out war would develop.

Pearson's Plan

Lester Pearson, Canadian Secretary of State for External Affairs, proposed a solution for this crisis. In a speech to the UN's General Assembly on November 1, 1956, Pearson said that a ceasefire agreement could be arrived at. He recommended forming "a UN force large enough to keep these borders at peace while a political settlement is being worked out." He also offered Canadian help in creating such a force.

Pearson's speech marked the first mention in international diplomacy of a UN peacekeeping force. As a direct result of Pearson's suggestion, the United Nations Emergency Force (UNEF) was formed, the famous "blue berets" who have been at the centre of all the UN's peacekeeping efforts ever since. This force is made up of soldiers from countries who are not directly involved in the dispute. They are not supposed to fight unless under attack. The first commander of UNEF was a Canadian, General E.M.L. Burns.

Figure 35-1 The Middle East at the time of the Suez Crisis in 1956.

BIOGRAPHY

A NEW STAR IS BORN

Subject: Lester B. Pearson

Dates: 1897-1972

Most Notable Accomplishments: Won the Nobel Peace Prize in 1957 and served as Prime Minister of Canada from 1963 to 1968.

Thumbnail Sketch: Born in Toronto, Lester Pearson served in the Royal Flying Corps during World War I. He was educated at the University of Toronto and at Oxford University in England, teaching history at U of T from 1924 to 1928. After this he was made the first Secretary of the newly formed Department of External Affairs. He was a member of the conference that formed the United Nations in 1945.

From 1945 to 1946, Pearson served as Canadian Ambassador to the United States. From 1946 to 1948, he was Under Secretary of State for External Affairs and a frequent spokesman for Canada at the UN. In 1952, he was named President of the General Assembly, and he chaired the Security Council in 1957. A devoted Liberal, Pearson led his party to power in 1963 and served as Prime Minister until 1968.

Significant Quote: "Diplomacy is letting someone else have your way."

Figure 35-3 As a result of his efforts in setting up the UN's peacekeeping force, Lester Pearson was awarded the Nobel Peace Prize in 1957. This award set in motion a wave of pride that spread across Canada, as this editorial cartoon shows.

CultureLink

THE BIRTH OF CANADA'S FLAG

During the Suez Crisis, Canada planned to send infantry to join the UN peacekeeping force. Egypt, however, objected to this idea. The Canadian uniforms, badges, flags, and regimental names were all too much like those of the British invaders, said the Egyptians. Under the circumstances, it would be impossible for the Egyptians to believe the Canadians were impartial.

The soldiers in the Canadian contingent of the UN force were replaced by service and supply personnel, who did not wear uniforms. This experience convinced Lester Pearson that Canada needed its own set of symbols. In 1964, when Pearson was Prime Minister, Canada got its distinctive maple leaf flag.

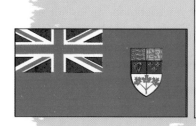

Figure 35-4 Canada's flag, with the single red maple leaf and two red bars, received royal approval on January 28, 1965. Before that, Canada used the "Red Ensign," shown on the left. Can you tell why the Egyptians thought this looked too much like the British Union Jack?

RECONNECT

1. Explain in your own words why Gamal Nasser decided to nationalize the Suez Canal.

2. The plan for the UN's peacekeeping force originated in Canada, one of the countries known as a **middle power** on the world stage. Do you think the plan would have been accepted if it had come from one of the "superpowers," that is, the United States or the Soviet Union?

FOCUS

This section will help you understand
a. why foreign aid is necessary
b. the benefits of foreign aid to the receiver and to the giver.

> "Give me a fish today, and I will be hungry tomorrow. Teach me how to fish, and I will never be hungry again.
> —Chinese proverb.

Why Is Foreign Aid Necessary?

In the early 1990s, Canada gave away about $3 billion a year in foreign aid. About $430 million of this annual figure was in food aid, more than any other country in the world. Many Canadians wonder why we should be so generous. The answer is that there are countries in the world that have far fewer resources than Canada and are not as economically developed. Foreign aid is based on the idea that the wealthier nations of the world should help the nations in need.

The most serious problem facing developing countries is the lack of a diversified economy. This means that they tend to produce only one or two products, usually raw materials such as minerals or food products like coffee. When the demand for such a product falls, so does its price. The developing country finds it is unable to earn enough money to support its people. Also, it cannot afford to buy expensive finished goods, such as farm machinery, that might help improve its economy in the long run. A vicious cycle sets in, and the people start to lose hope that they will ever be able to climb out of their poverty.

The goal of foreign aid is to help developing countries to become economically self-sufficient.

Figure 36-1 Until it was closed in 1995, Manila's garbage dump served as home to thousands of people. The dump was called Smokey Mountain because of the fires that burned in it and never went out, fed by methane gas from decomposing garbage. The residents of Smokey Mountain supported themselves by scavenging still-useful articles from the dump. What their lives were like is difficult for most Canadians to imagine. Eliminating this sort of poverty is one of the goals of Canada's foreign aid program.

MOTIVES FOR GIVING AID		
Humanitarian	**Economic**	**Political**
Wealthy people should help people who are less well-off, and the same principle applies among nations. This is the basis of charity. It is the same idea behind charitable organizations such as the United Way and the Salvation Army.	Poor countries cannot afford to buy the goods manufactured by rich countries. If rich countries want to expand their markets, they must help the poor countries improve their economies.	When Canada gives aid to another country, we hope that country will support us in world affairs. A prosperous country is less likely to endure rebellions, dictatorships, and wars.

Figure 36-2 There are several reasons for giving foreign aid to needy countries. Sometimes foreign aid can benefit the country that gives it almost as much as the country that receives it.

The Colombo Plan

Canada's foreign aid program did not really begin until 1950. In that year, Canada, along with the other member countries in the British Commonwealth, met at Colombo, capital of Sri Lanka. There Commonwealth members hammered out a plan through which the wealthier members would contribute to a fund for the benefit of the poorer Commonwealth nations.

Canada's initial contribution was $10 million, which was sent to India in the form of food products. Eventually, the plan was extended so that it benefited even those poor nations that did not belong to the Commonwealth. Over the years, Canada has contributed more than $2 billion to the Colombo Plan.

Figure 36-3
Much of the money Canada has contributed to the Colombo plan has gone to India. This is a photo of Bombay, where almost 50% of the city's nine million inhabitants live in slums or on sidewalks.

FOREIGN AID BY COUNTRY, 1995				
Country	**Amount of Aid in $U.S.,1995**	**% of GNP**		**Per Capita ($U.S.)**
		1984/85	**1995**	
Australia	1 194 000 000	0.47	0.36	$62
Canada	2 067 000 000	0.50	0.38	$73
France	8 443 000 000	0.62	0.55	$137
Germany	7 524 000 000	0.46	0.31	$81
Japan	14 489 000 000	0.31	0.28	$106
Netherlands	3 226 000 000	0.97	0.81	$172
Norway	1 244 000 000	1.02	0.87	$255
Sweden	1 704 000 000	0.83	0.77	$189
Switzerland	1 804 000 000	0.30	0.34	$135
United Kingdom	3 157 000 000	0.33	0.28	$53
United States	7 367 000 000	0.24	0.10	$33

Source: United Nations Development Program, Human Development Report *(New York: Oxford University Press, 1997), p. 214.*

Figure 36-4 The United Nations recommends that developed nations set aside 0.7% of their gross national product (GNP) for foreign aid. That means that for every $100 a nation produces in goods and services, it should give 70 cents to foreign aid. Which of the countries listed above actually meet that goal?

Aid for Africa

More than any other region in the developing world, Africa and its problems have been highlighted in the media over the past several years. Many of the continent's problems are rooted in the severe food shortages it has suffered since the 1960s. About 40% of Canada's foreign aid is sent to Africa.

Africa's problems go back to the time when many of its countries were colonies of European powers, especially England, France, Portugal, and Belgium. The Europeans exploited their colonies as sources of cheap raw materials. Production of raw materials for European factories was considered more important than food production, which became inefficient. When the prices of their raw materials went down on the world market, the African countries became even poorer. They were plagued by three problems: poor health, poor education, and poor agriculture.

In 1986 the Canadian government started a 15-year program called Africa 2000. This program has a special fund of $150 million and is designed to provide assistance in three ways:

▶ by funding agricultural research,

▶ by fighting drought, and

▶ by promoting African self-sufficiency in food production.

CaseStudy

CITIES AND POVERTY

Even in a country as wealthy as Canada, there are many problems associated with life in large cities: homelessness, crime, and poverty are just a few. In the quickly growing cities of the developing countries, the problems are even worse. Consider the plight of Mexico City, which by the year 2000 will have a population of 28 million:

- thousands of people from the countryside stream into the already overcrowded city every day.
- about 10% of current residents have no running water.
- about 15% of current residents have no sewage facilities.
- only about 50% of the garbage produced in the city on a given day can be picked up and processed.

Mexico City is not alone in its inability to deal with its population explosion. Throughout the developing world, cities are growing at an unprecedented rate. Consider the two tables below. In 1980 six of the world's 10 largest cities were in industrialized countries such as the United States and Japan. Only four were in developing countries. By 2000, the situation will be reversed, with six of the largest cities in the world in developing countries, which, like Mexico, will not have the resources to deal with them.

The Ten Largest Cities in the World, 1980 and 2000

1980

City	Population (in millions)
New York, U.S.A.	16.5
Tokyo-Yokohama, Japan	14.4
Mexico City, Mexico	14.0
Los Angeles-Long Beach, U.S.A.	10.6
Shanghai, China	10.0
Buenos Aires, Argentina	9.7
Paris, France	8.5
Moscow, U.S.S.R.	8.0
Beijing, China	8.0
Chicago, U.S.A.	7.7

2000 (projected)

City	Population (in millions)
Tokyo-Yokohama, Japan	30.0
Mexico City, Mexico	27.9
Sao Paulo, Brazil	25.4
Seoul, South Korea	22.0
Bombay, India	15.4
New York, U.S.A.	14.7
Osaka-Kobe-Kyoto, Japan	14.3
Tehran, Iran	14.3
Rio de Janiero, Brazil	14.2
Calcutta, India	14.1

Sources: United Nations (1995) and U.S. Bureau of the Census (1995).

In Canada, in addition to government aid, there are some non-governmental organizations (NGOs) that work to eliminate problems in cities of the developing world. Here are three examples:

- **Watercan** Set up by 80-year-old Michael Lubbock, Watercan raises funds in Canada for developing safe water projects around the world. The World Health Organization estimates that 80% of the disease in developing countries is due to inadequate water supply and sanitation. Each year about 25 million people die from the effects of contaminated water, 15 million of them children.
- **Rooftops Canada Foundation** An organization designed to inform interested people about housing issues in the developing world. It also raises funds for housing projects in those countries.
- **Federation of Canadian Municipalities** This organization was set up in 1987 as an international program to establish relationships with cities in other parts of the world. For example, Toronto has been paired with Sao Paulo, Brazil, and Vancouver with Guangzhou, China.

The UN also has special programs for Africa. In developing these programs, the UN has listened to recommendations from the African nations themselves. African aid programs call for:

► combating food emergencies
► developing agriculture
► developing industries related to agriculture
► developing strategies for drought
► stressing education: everyone should be able to read and write.

Women in the Developing World

Mahatma Gandhi once said: "If you educate a man, you educate an individual. If you educate a woman, you educate the whole family." Statistics tell us that a woman who reads and writes will have children who grow up literate, will have healthier babies, and will have fewer babies.

Unfortunately, this is not the case for many women in the developing world. They are often poorly educated or not educated at all. This means that they work 18-hour days in low-paid jobs or as servants. Ironically, these women also produce 50% of all the food, fetch the water and firewood, and look after the children. They are the glue that holds their families together.

In recognition that women are of fundamental importance to the progress of a society, the Canadian government now requires all aid projects to include a WID sheet. WID stands for Women in Development, and the sheet has to show what effects the aid will have on women specifically. If there is no obvious benefit for women, the project is sent back for rethinking.

The UN also has a program for women in developing countries called UNIFEM, the United Nations Development Fund for Women. This is the only UN program that is aimed solely at women.

Figure 36-5 Drilling for water in Niger under a plan sponsored by the Canadian International Development Agency (CIDA).

STATSCAN   A World Apart

If you had been born an average African instead of a Canadian, life would look very different:

• you would have one chance in three of drinking safe water,
• you would use only 4% as much energy,
• you would have one chance in five of owning a radio, and one in 50 of owning a television,
• your country would be 1/17th as wealthy as Canada,
• your children would be 12 times as likely to die of infant diseases,
• you would have 1/19th the chance of seeing a doctor,
• $7 per year would be spent on your health and education, instead of $1299.

Source: Canadian International Development Agency, On Africa: Development (Ottawa: Ministry of Supply and Services, Sept. 1987).

Figure 36-6 A woman field worker in Zimbabwe.

RECONNECT

1. Offer three reasons why many nations require foreign aids.

2. Do you support Canada's foreign aid efforts? Explain your views in detail.

FOCUS

This section will help you understand
a. what the Commonwealth of Nations is
b. which nations belong to it.

What Is the Commonwealth?

If you are a student in one of Canada's larger cities, chances are your school has a multicultural population. This means that the families of the students in the school come from different countries around the world. If you inquired, you would find out that most of these countries belong to the Commonwealth of Nations.

Look at the map in Figure 37-1, which shows the 51 Commonwealth countries around the world. What do these countries have in common? They were all at one time members of the British Empire. Now they are independent, self-governing nations that belong voluntarily to the Commonwealth. They also have in common the use of the English language and similar systems of law and parliamentary government. The British monarch, Queen Elizabeth, is the head of the Commonwealth, but her role is purely ceremonial.

Together, the Commonwealth countries contain 25% of the world's population. This means that if all these countries work together they can accomplish a great deal. Unlike the United Nations, the Commonwealth does not have a charter, but in 1971 the Commonwealth made a declaration of four principles:

▶ to cooperate in furthering world peace,
▶ to guarantee the personal freedoms of its citizens,
▶ to ensure racial equality, and
▶ to lessen differences in wealth by working for the economic development of member countries.

When the Commonwealth meets, each country is treated equally. The smallest state has as much of a say as the largest.

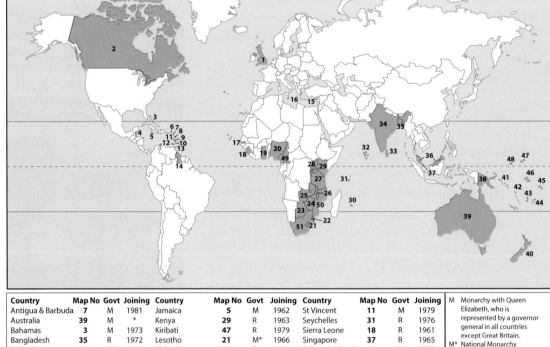

Country	Map No	Govt	Joining	Country	Map No	Govt	Joining	Country	Map No	Govt	Joining
Antigua & Barbuda	7	M	1981	Jamaica	5	M	1962	St Vincent	11	M	1979
Australia	39	M	*	Kenya	29	R	1963	Seychelles	31	R	1976
Bahamas	3	M	1973	Kiribati	47	R	1979	Sierra Leone	18	R	1961
Bangladesh	35	R	1972	Lesotho	21	M*	1966	Singapore	37	R	1965
Barbados	10	M	1966	Malawi	26	R	1964	Solomon Islands	41	M	1978
Belize	4	M	1981	Malaysia	36	M*	1957	South Africa	51	R	1993
Botswana	23	M	1966	Maldives	32	R	1982	Sri Lanka	33	R	1948
Camaroons	49	R	1995	Malta	16	R	1964	Swaziland	22	M*	1968
Canada	2	M	*	Mauritius	30	M	1968	Tanzania	27	R	1961
Cyprus	15	R	1961	Mozambique	50	R	1995	Tonga	44	M*	1970
Dominica	8	R	1978	Nauru	48	R	1968	Trinidad & Tobago	13	R	1962
Fiji	43	M	1970	New Zealand	40	M	*	Tuvalu	46	M	1978
The Gambia	17	R	1965	Nigeria	20	R	1960	Uganda	28	R	1962
Ghana	19	R	1957	Papua New Guinea	38	M	1975	United Kingdom	1	M	
Grenada	12	M	1974	St Kitts & Nevis	6	M	1983	Vanuatu	42	R	1980
Guyana	14	R	1966	(St Christopher)				Western Samoa	45	R	1970
India	34	R	1947	St Lucia	9	M	1979	Zambia	25	R	1964
								Zimbabwe	24	R	1980

Map adapted from information supplied by Commonwealth Secretariat.

M Monarchy with Queen Elizabeth, who is represented by a governor general in all countries except Great Britain.
M* National Monarchy
R Republic
* Statute of Westminster (1931)

Maldives, Nauru, St Vincent and Tuvalu are special members. They participate in functional meetings and activities, but do not attend meetings of Heads of Government.

Small islands are slightly exaggerated in size.

Figure 37-1 The Commonwealth countries of the world. Which are the three largest countries by physical size in the Commonwealth?

Canada's Role

Because of its size and economic strength, Canada has always played a leading role in the Commonwealth. Canadian Prime Minister John Diefenbaker condemned South Africa in 1961 for its policy of **apartheid**. This led directly to South Africa's departure from the Commonwealth and to an economic boycott of that country by Commonwealth nations. The boycott lasted until 1994, when South Africa renounced apartheid and Nelson Mandela was elected the country's president.

When the first permanent office for the Commonwealth was set up in London, England in 1964, a Canadian diplomat named Arnold Smith became the Commonwealth's first secretary-general. Canada is also the main contributor to the Commonwealth's programs. For instance, Canada provides more than 40% of the budget for the Commonwealth Fund for Technical Assistance, which is the organization's main agency for giving aid to developing countries.

The Commonwealth has provided Canada with excellent opportunities for extending its influence around the world.

The Commonwealth Games

Like the Olympics, the Commonwealth Games are a worldwide event held every four years. The privilege of serving as host to the Games rotates among the different Commonwealth countries. Canada served as the original host country in 1930, when the Games (then known as the Empire Games) were held in Hamilton, Ontario. The 1954 Commonwealth Games were held in Victoria, B.C. These games won world-wide attention when the only two runners to have clocked a four-minute mile up to that point competed against each other. After a slow start, Roger Bannister narrowly defeated John Landy in one of the great races of the 20th century.

In 1978 the Games were held in Edmonton, and Canada won an unheard-of total of 109 medals. Great Britain was next in line with 87. Over the years, the Games have provided an opportunity for the millions of young people in the Commonwealth to better understand the role the organization plays in developing world peace and cooperation among nations.

The Commonwealth Games, like the Commonwealth itself, have proven that people of different races, religions, and economic conditions can work together for a common good.

N ε T S u ʀ ꟻ ε ʀ

THE COMMONWEALTH OF LEARNING

Many Commonwealth countries need to improve the education of their children to ensure a brighter future for them. Often, however, there is not enough money or the facilities to do this. So in 1988 the Commonwealth of Learning was founded to give this sort of help. This organization is based in Vancouver, and its purpose is to provide better educational opportunities through cooperation between Commonwealth countries.

Most often, this is done through "distance education," using the most modern communication technologies to bring education to those who would not normally have access to it. Some of the methods used are:

- satellites
- desktop publishing
- tele-conferencing
- the Internet.

THE COMMONWEALTH OF LEARNING'S WEB SITE CAN BE FOUND AT: http://www.col.org

FOCUS

a. Make a list of things the Commonwealth nations have in common.
b. Give two reasons why Canada has played such a prominent role in the Commonwealth.

FOCUS

This section will help you understand
  a. what the aims of La Francophonie are and which countries belong to it
  b. what these countries have in common.

The International French Community

Canada belongs to several large international organizations such as the United Nations and the Commonwealth. Since Canada has such a strong French identity (6.6 million Canadians speak French as their mother tongue), it also belongs to La Francophonie, a worldwide organization founded in 1970 that emphasizes the importance of French language and culture.

La Francophonie has more than 40 member nations forming an international community of more than 120 million people. Members hold summits every two years to discuss issues of common interest. The first major gathering of member countries was held in 1970 in Niger. Since many of the countries are from the developing world, economic matters usually receive much attention. Things that a poor country cannot do on its own, can often be accomplished through cooperation and a pooling of resources. For instance, wealthier nations such as Canada and France can help poorer nations such as Haiti and Burkina Faso. Cooperation also occurs in the areas of education, culture, science, and technology.

One of La Francophonie's major concerns is the same as that in Quebec: how to preserve French language and culture in a world that is increasingly dominated by the English language. It was only after pressure from La Francophonie, that the Olympic Games recognized the importance of French and started making announcements in two languages, French and English.

Canada is a full member of La Francophonie, and the governments of Quebec and New Brunswick are also members because they represent large French-speaking populations.

TV5

Perhaps the most visible accomplishment of La Francophonie has been the creation of TV5. This is the international French-language television channel that started broadcasting in 1983. Shown in North America, the Caribbean, Europe, and Africa, it brings to its audiences news and entertainment in the French language. The purpose of TV5, however, goes beyond entertainment. It provides a means of communication and cooperation among peoples who share the use of the French language.

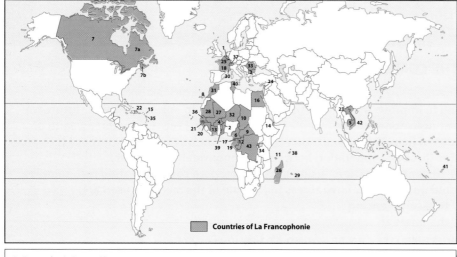

Countries of La Francophonie

La Francophonie Country List

1 Belgium	8 Cape Verde	17 Equatorial Guinea	26 Madagascar	35 Saint Lucia
2 Benin	9 Central African Republic	18 France	27 Mali	36 Senegal
3 Bulgaria	10 Chad	19 Gabon	28 Mauritania	37 Switzerland
4 Burkina Faso	11 Comoros	20 Guinea	29 Mauritius	38 The Seychelles
5 Cambodia	12 Congo	21 Guinea-Bissau	30 Monaco	39 Togo
6 Cameroon	13 Cote D'Ivoire	22 Haiti	31 Morocco	40 Tunisia
7 Canada	14 Djibuti	23 Laos	32 Niger	41 Vanuatu
7a Quebec	15 Dominica	24 Lebanon	33 Romania	42 Vietnam
7b New Brunswick	16 Egypt	25 Luxembourg	34 Rwanda	43 Zaire

Figure 38-1 The member states of La Francophonie.

CultureLink

FLAGS OF FRANCOPHONE
COMMUNITIES IN CANADA

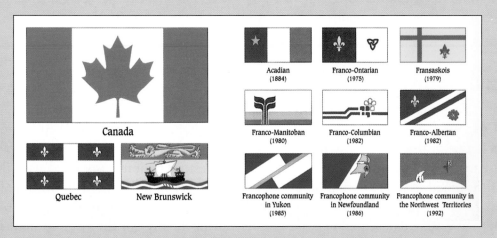

Canada

Acadian
(1884)

Franco-Ontarian
(1975)

Fransaskois
(1979)

Franco-Manitoban
(1980)

Franco-Columbian
(1982)

Franco-Albertan
(1982)

Quebec

New Brunswick

Francophone community
in Yukon
(1985)

Francophone community
in Newfoundland
(1986)

Francophone community in
the Northwest Territories
(1992)

Figure 38-2 Membership in La Francophonie helps to make the world aware of the special nature of Canada and gives francophone Canadians a chance to have an influence in many regions of the world.

While most Canadian Francophones live in Quebec, about one million live in other provinces and territories. The largest of these other communities is in New Brunswick, but there are nine other francophone communities across Canada.

Quebec takes particular pride in participating in this organization. La Francophonie helps to reinforce Quebec's sense of its unique cultural identity when surrounded by a larger English culture in Canada and the United States.

Today, through the use of cable technology, TV5 reaches 1.6 million people in Quebec, 3.4 million in the rest of Canada, and about 3 million in the United States. TV5 is a showcase for Canadian artists, since many of TV5's shows are produced in Canada. In return for their contribution, Canadians are able to see European programming that they wouldn't otherwise have access to.

Canada has also greatly helped in TV5's expansion into Africa, where more than 20 countries are members of La Francophonie. TV5 has enjoyed a great deal of success in Africa, where many of the colour televisions receive only one station and the broadcasting authorities have reserved that station for TV5. In these places TV5 enjoys the privilege of opening the world to its viewers.

Figure 38-3 The logo of La Francophonie. The round shape was designed to give a sense of universality and energetic advancement. The bands are in five colours and indicate cooperation and mutual assistance. These five colours also represent the colours of all the flags of the member countries, and the five continents on which they are found.

RECONNECT

1. Why is La Francophonie particularly important in a country like Canada?

2. As a student in a country that is officially bilingual, how important is the French language and culture to you? Explain.

FOCUS

This section will help you understand
  a. what flashpoints are
  b. where and why some major flashpoints have occurred since 1945.

What Is a Flashpoint?

In science, the word "flashpoint" refers to the temperature at which vapour from oil or some other substance will catch fire in the air. By extension, the word is also used to refer to conflicts between nations that have threatened to ignite into another world war. Several of these flashpoints occurred between 1945 and 1989, the dates marking the beginning and end of the Cold War.

The Berlin Blockade, 1948

Right up to 1989, Berlin was at the very centre of the Cold War. At the close of World War II, the victorious Allies divided Germany into four zones. Each zone was under the control of a different Ally—the United States, Great Britain, France, and the Soviet Union. Berlin, the former capital of Germany, was completely in the Soviet sector. It too was divided into four zones controlled by the same four nations. To give the Western nations access to West Berlin, a corridor existed for transportation.

In June 1948, the Soviets tried to force the Western nations out of Berlin by cutting off all rail, road, and water links between the city and West Germany. The people of West Berlin were in danger of starving.

The Western nations responded with the Berlin Airlift. Over 11 months and with the aid of 277 728 flights, tonnes of food were delivered to the city. The Soviets finally got the message and lifted the blockade in May 1949.

The Berlin Wall

If people around the world who lived through the Cold War had to choose a single artifact that best symbolized the divisions of that time, most would probably choose the Berlin Wall.

When Germany was divided after the war, the difference in the standard of living between East and West Germany soon became obvious. West Germany was relatively wealthy and had plenty of consumer goods and jobs. East Germany suffered severe shortages. By 1961 some three million East Germans had fled to the west. These people tended to be well educated and well trained, so there was a "brain drain" in East Germany and its economy grew even weaker.

The leaders of East Germany responded with a cinder-block wall 28 miles long, topped with barbed wire, and guarded by soldiers armed with machine-guns. Construction began at midnight on Sunday, August 13, 1961. Over the years 191 East Germans were killed trying to cross the Wall and 5000 others captured. Another 5000

Figure 39-1 The Berlin Airlift.

EyeWitness

In 1997, newspapers around the world carried stories of two former East German border guards who were convicted of manslaughter in the death of a teenager 35 years earlier. The victim, Peter Fechter, had been shot down as he tried to scale the Berlin Wall.

Berlin Wall guards convicted

BERLIN (Reuter)—Two former East German border guards were convicted of manslaughter yesterday for the 1962 killing of a teenager who bled to death at the Berlin Wall as his cries went unheeded. The two-day trial could not determine which guard fired the fatal shot that killed Peter Fechter, Judge Hans-Juergen Schaal said. But he ruled in a Berlin court that both guards were still guilty of manslaughter.

They were given suspended sentences following a pattern established in previous trials involving shootings at the wall.

"It is legally irrelevant that it could not be proven that either of the guards fired the deadly shot," Schaal said. "Joint manslaughter was committed here because neither of you consciously tried to miss the target."

Fechter was hit in the pelvis while running toward the Berlin Wall near an Allied checkpoint. He called in vain for help for about 50 minutes as he slowly bled to death.

Of all the people killed at the Berlin Wall that divided the city during the Cold War, Fechter's agonized death was the most famous.

The East German guards did not provide first aid because there was no senior officer on duty in that section of the Wall who had the authority to order assistance. West Berlin police and Western Allies tried vainly to help by tossing first aid kits over the Wall.

Fechter climbed through a window in an East Berlin building, jumped over a line of barbed wire and ran toward the Wall. He was just 10 metres away when a bullet hit him.

Source: The Toronto Star, *March 6, 1997, p. A21.*

Figure 39-2 The Berlin Wall.

succeeded in making it over (or under) the Wall. The Western powers protested vehemently against the Wall's construction but did nothing else to stop it. The Wall remained in place until November 9, 1989, when the government of East Germany opened its borders to West Germany.

The Vietnam War

Vietnam was part of a French colony called Indochina, which also included Laos and Cambodia. In 1954, the North Vietnamese army under Ho Chi Minh overran the French Foreign Legion's fortress at Dien Bien Phu, killing or capturing the entire garrison of 16 000 soldiers. A peace conference followed at Geneva, Switzerland, and an agreement was signed that divided Vietnam in two at the 17th parallel. This was supposed to be a temporary arrangement until free elections could be held to reunite the two parts. The North had a Communist government, and the South an anti-Communist government. The elections never took place. The division became permanent and hostilities grew eventually into **guerrilla warfare**.

The U.S. became involved in the war partly because of the domino theory, which stated that if one country in an area fell to the Communists, then all of its neighbours would also collapse. Although U.S. involvement in the early 1960s was minor, by 1968 there were almost 500 000 U.S. troops in Vietnam. As the U.S. increased its support for the South, the Chinese and Soviets sent more supplies to the North.

Neither side made permanent gains. As the casualties rose, the American people turned against the war. In 1973 a cease-fire was signed and U.S. forces began to withdraw. By 1976, all of Vietnam was under Communist control.

Although Canadian troops were not involved in the fighting, the Canadian government was part of an international commission set up in 1954 whose job was to oversee the cease-fire after the defeat of the French.

The Cuban Missile Crisis

Those who lived through the Cuban Missile Crisis remember it as a time when many people thought the world was about to end in a nuclear holocaust. The crisis developed as a result of poor relations between the U.S. on one side and Cuba and the Soviet Union on the other. In 1958 Fidel Castro overthrew the government of Fulgencio Batista and in 1959 set up a Communist government on the island. In 1961 the American Central Intelligence Agency sponsored an invasion of Cuba by 1500 Cuban exiles. The newly elected president John F. Kennedy refused to provide the promised air support, and the "invasion" turned into a complete rout of the exile forces.

Figure 39-3   U.S. troops carry their wounded away from a battle zone in Vietnam in 1968.

In 1962 Kennedy learned that the Soviets were building missile bases in Cuba. Photos taken from U-2 reconnaissance planes showed that some missiles were already in place. U.S. military experts feared that these missiles would be equipped with nuclear warheads.

Because Cuba was only 145 kilometres from the U.S. border, Kennedy found this situation intolerable. He decided on a showdown with the leader of the Soviet Union, Nikita Krushchev, even though he knew this might provoke a war. All U.S. forces were put on full alert and on October 22, 1962, Kennedy went on television and accused the Soviets of creating a threat to world peace. He also said that the U.S. would begin a naval and air blockade of Cuba to stop any further shipments from the Soviet Union. The blockade was to stay in effect until the missiles were removed.

At the same time the Canadian government put its forces on alert, and Canadian bases were ready to accept American planes as part of the NORAD agreement. Frantic negotiations took place to avert what seemed like certain nuclear catastrophe. On October 28 Krushchev announced that because the U.S. had agreed not to invade Cuba, he had ordered the missiles to be removed. The world breathed a collective sigh of relief.

Figure 39-4   One of the photos taken by U.S. reconnaissance aircraft showing Cuban missile bases under construction. This photo helped to spark the Cuban Missile Crisis in 1961.

BIOGRAPHY

Subject: John F. Kennedy

Dates: 1917-1963

Most Notable Accomplishment: Served as the 35th president of the United States, at 43 the youngest man ever elected to that position.

Thumbnail Sketch: Kennedy was born into a wealthy Boston family. He went to Harvard University, and when the U.S. entered World War II, he served with distinction in the Navy. After the war, he entered politics and was elected to Congress in 1957. In 1960 Kennedy narrowly defeated Richard Nixon for the presidency. As president, Kennedy started the Peace Corps, vowed that a U.S. citizen would be the first person on the moon before the decade ended, and increased the American military presence in Vietnam. On Novemeber 22, 1963, Kennedy was assassinated in Dallas Texas.

Figure 39-5   John. F. Kennedy

Significant Quote: "It shall be the policy of this nation to regard any nuclear missile launched from Cuba against any nation in the Western hemisphere as an attack by the Soviet Union on the United States requiring a full retaliatory response upon the Soviet Union."
—*John F. Kennedy in an address to the United States, October 22, 1961.*

BIOGRAPHY

Subject: Nikita Krushchev

Dates: 1894-1971

Most Notable Accomplishment: Served as premier of the Soviet Union from 1958 to 1964.

Thumbnail Sketch: Nikita Krushchev was born into a poor family in the Ukraine, and as a young man did not receive a very good education. He joined the Bolshevik party in 1918 and fought in the Red Army. Krushchev worked in various bureaucratic positions during the 1920s and '30s, rising quickly in the Party ranks.

After Josef Stalin's death in 1953, Krushchev became leader of the Communist Party, and in 1956 he launched a famous attack on the excesses of the Stalinist era, when millions of people were executed or sent to labour camps.

Figure 39-6   Nikita Krushchev.

In 1958 Krushchev became premier of the Soviet Union. He had an impulsive personality. In his policies, he veered between promoting the idea of "peaceful coexistence" with the U.S. and arranging confrontations like the Berlin Wall and the Cuban Missile Crisis. In 1964 he was forced to resign as premier, partly because of the embarrassment the Soviet Union suffered as a result of the Missile Crisis.

Significant Quote: "We sent the Americans a note saying that we agreed to remove our missiles and bombers on the condition that the President give us his assurances that there would be no invasion of Cuba by the forces of the United States or anybody else. Finally Kennedy gave in and agreed to make a statement giving us such an assurance...

"The Caribbean crisis was a triumph of Soviet foreign policy and a personal triumph in my own career... We achieved, I would say, a spectacular success without having to fire a single shot!"
—*Nikita Krushchev, quoted in* Krushchev Remembers, *ed. E. Crankshaw.*

RECONNECT

1. Why was Berlin at the very centre of the Cold War?

2. What was the connection between the Cold War and the Cuban Missile Crisis. Be specific in your reply.

FOCUS

This section will help you understand
a. the causes of the Gulf War
b. Canada's contributions to the United Nations' peacemaking effort.

Operation Desert Storm

As you can see by looking at the map of the Persian Gulf in Figure 40-1, Iraq's access to the sea is limited by Kuwait. The Iraqi government has disputed its border with Kuwait for the last 50 years. In the late 1980s, the two countries were negotiating to try and resolve their border dispute. In 1990, the negotiations collapsed and Iraq invaded Kuwait on August 1. The Kuwaiti government went into exile immediately, and the people were subjected to violence and abuse.

The UN reacted by condemning Iraq and its leader Saddam Hussein. It also imposed an economic boycott on Iraq, but Hussein refused to order his army out of Kuwait. At this point, the United States felt more decisive action was necessary. On November 29, 1990, the UN issued Resolution 678, which authorized the use of "all means necessary" to force Iraq out of Kuwait. The resulting military action was called Desert Storm.

A combined military force called the Multinational Force (MNF) attacked the Iraqi army for six weeks. The MNF killed some 120 000 Iraqis and eventually pushed them out of Kuwait and a good part of the way back to Baghdad, Iraq's capital. By the end of the six-week period, the Iraqi army had been crushed by the MNF's superior technology. Of the MNF forces, about 200 soldiers had been killed.

On February 27, 1991, U.S. President George Bush called for a cease-fire. Instead of mounting a full-scale invasion of Iraq, the MNF let the surviving parts of Iraq's army retreat to Baghdad. Some critics felt this decision failed to solve the problem of Iraqi aggression in the Middle East. Iraq did have to pay war damages, and the UN forced Saddam to destroy stockpiles of chemical and biological weapons.

Canada's War Effort

Canada's main contribution to the MNF was in ships and aircraft. Three Canadian ships left Halifax, Nova Scotia on August 24, 1990, arriving one month later in the Persian Gulf. Their assignment was to patrol the shipping lanes in the Gulf. They were to stop and search any ship suspected of carrying supplies to Iraq.

Canada also sent a squadron of CF-18 fighter planes. At first these planes were only supposed to protect the Canadian ships. Later, however, they were allowed to take on an offensive role in the war, escorting coalition bombers and attacking ground targets. This was the first time Canadian planes had participated in a war in 46 years, since the Korean War.

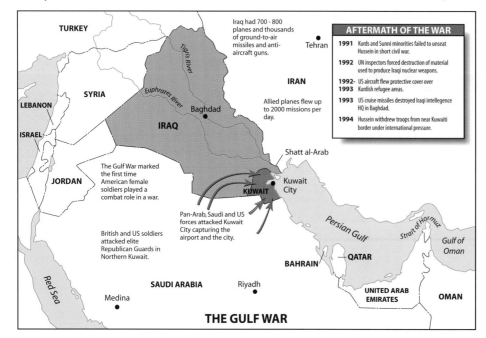

Figure 40-1 The Persian Gulf area at the time of the Gulf War.

CultureLink

THE DIFFERENCE BETWEEN PEACEMAKING AND PEACEKEEPING

When it intervenes in conflicts between nations, the UN can play one of two distinct roles, either as a peacemaker or a peacekeeper. **Peacemaking** usually involves UN troops directly in armed combat. It is designed to bring peace to the affected region by pushing the conflicting parties to the negotiating table. The UN played peace-making roles in Korea in the 1950s and in the Gulf War in 1991.

In a **peacekeeping** operation, UN troops are deployed only after a truce or ceasefire agreement has been reached between nations or groups at war with each other. The UN troops are there to monitor the ceasefire and to ensure that new fighting does not break out before a lasting peace settlement can be finalized. The UN played a peacekeeping role in the Suez in 1956 and in the former Yugoslavia in 1992.

Figure 40-2 Canadian Forces ground crew lift a Sidewinder heat-seeking missile before attaching it to a CF-18 fighter jet. This photo was taken at an airbase in Qatar during the Gulf War. By this time, Canadian pilots were aggressively attacking targets in Kuwait and Iraq.

Figure 40-3 As the Iraqi army was being pushed out of Kuwait, Saddam Hussein ordered his troops to blow up hundreds of oil wells. The resulting fires burned out of control, sending up enormous clouds of acrid smoke. Not only was this an environmental disaster, but oil was the mainstay of the Kuwaiti economy.

RECONNECT

1. Why did the UN engage in military operations against Iraq?

2. What role did Canadians play in the Gulf War?

FOCUS

This section will help you understand
a. how the collapse of the Somalian government led to civil war and UN intervention
b. the origins of the Somalia Inquiry in Canada.

Clan Warfare

Civil war broke out in Somalia in late 1990 when local **clans** overthrew the corrupt government of General Mohamed Siad Barre. This left the country with no central government. The clan leaders who had ousted the dictatorship had long-standing feuds with each other, and soon open warfare erupted. In the chaos that followed, about 30 000 people were killed and hundreds of thousands faced famine and starvation.

Figure 41-1
Somali famine victims at a food-distribution site set up during Operation Restore Hope.

Operation Restore Hope

The international community decided to take action. For the first time in its history the UN used its powers of intervention without being invited to by the country involved. This action was called Operation Restore Hope and involved 30 000 troops from 20 countries, the majority coming from the U.S.

Operation Restore Hope had two goals:
▶ to bring peace to the country by disarming the clans, and
▶ to get food to the starving.

Figure 41-2 Several U.S. soldiers on the UN force were killed after relations soured between General Aideed and the UN. A series of anti-U.S. protests in Mogadishu further eroded U.S. support for the mission.

When UN troops first arrived in April 1992, things went well enough. Then the UN decided to throw its support behind one of the most powerful clan leaders, General Mohammed Aideed. This angered the other clan leaders, and General Aideed himself grew angry when the UN demanded that he disarm his soldiers. Aideed ordered his forces to fire on the UN troops. The U.S. forces in Somalia put a price of $30 000 on Aideed's head. While trying to capture the general, U.S. troops killed several Somali civilians. The Somalis turned against the whole UN operation and killed a number of UN soldiers. The peacemaking venture was falling apart.

The last UN forces left Mogadishu, the capital of Somalia, in February 1995. Sporadic clan warfare continued, and in August 1996 General Aideed himself was killed. His son succeeded him as clan head, and it looked as if fighting between the clans would continue indefinitely.

There was widespread disappointment over the failure of the UN to accomplish the first of its objectives in Somalia, which was to bring peace. The UN did succeed, however in its second goal of relieving the famine that had threatened much of the population with starvation.

CaseStudy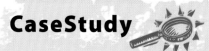

THE CANADIAN AIRBORNE REGIMENT AND THE SOMALIA AFFAIR

In April 1996, all 100 000 personnel in the Canadian Armed Forces were told to drop what-ever they were doing and search for any documents they could find that referred to events in Somalia three years earlier. The Somalia Affair was in the process of turning into the biggest scandal in the history of the Armed Forces. Before it was over, the Armed Forces would suffer the following indignities:

- the Canadian Airborne Regiment, one of the most "elite" of the Forces' units, would be disbanded, and its soldiers distributed among other regiments.
- General Jean Boyle, Commander-in Chief of the Armed Forces, would be forced to resign only 10 months after being appointed to that position.
- the Canadian public would learn that officials in the Armed Forces had illegally tampered with documents that referred to events in Somalia.
- the Somalia Inquiry would release a scathing report that blamed the Armed Forces for poor organization and failures of leadership.

What triggered the Somalia Inquiry and led to such disgrace for the Canadian Armed Forces?

When the Canadian government decided to assist in Operation Restore Hope, the Airborne Regiment was sent to a village in Somalia called Belet Huen. Despite the harsh con-ditions, poor food, and constant pilfering of supplies by young Somalis, the soldiers were credited with bringing peace to the region.

The image of the Airborne regiment as benevolent peacekeepers was to change permanently on the evening of March 16, 1993. The soldiers caught a young Somali named Shidane Abukar Arone inside the compound and took him to a hold-ing area. Three hours and fifteen minutes later, he was dead. Pictures published later in Canadian newspapers clearly showed that Arone had been tortured and died as the result of a prolonged beating.

One of the soldiers, Master Corporal Clayton Matchee, was charged with his death and arrested. Two days later guards found Matchee hanging in his cell. He survived but suffered such severe brain damage that he was unfit to stand trial. Private Kyle Brown, who witnessed and photographed the torture of Arone, was **court-martialled** and given a five-year prison sentence. Sergeant Mark Boland, who pleaded guilty to negligent performance of duty for not stopping the torture, was sentenced to 90 days in prison and demoted to private.

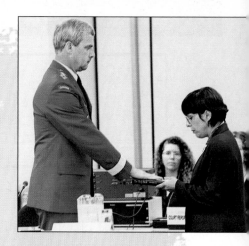

Figure 41-3 General Jean Boyle swears on the Bible before testifying at the Somalia Inquiry. General Boyle was the highest-ranking soldier to lose his position as a result of the Somalia Inquiry.

Figure 41-4 The Canadian Airborne Regiment in Somalia. The regiment was disbanded for its role in the Somalia Affair and a number of other scandals.

RECONNECT

1. The UN went into Somalia without being invited. The conditions were desperate, but did the threat of mass starvation justify an armed "invasion"?

2. What were the goals of Operation Restore Hope?

3. What was the "Somalia Affair?"

4. When the UN sends soldiers to a part of the world that is strange and unfamiliar to them, what efforts should the UN make to educate the soldiers about the society they will encounter there? Do you think such an education program could have stopped the soldiers in the Airborne Regiment from mistreating young Somalis?

FOCUS

This section will help you understand
  a. what the outlook is for Canada as a member of the world community in the 21st century.

The Past

In the first chapter of this book, we saw that 100 years ago Prime Minister Wilfrid Laurier made the following prediction: "As the 19th century belonged to the United States, so the 20th century will belong to Canada." Laurier spoke these words in a time of prosperity, when Canada's population and economy were growing rapidly. It was easy to be optimistic.

Did events during the 20th century bear out the Prime Minister's prediction? We have seen that Canada's optimistic outlook was shattered by World War I, when tens of thousands of Canadian soldiers died in the trenches. At the same time, the debate over conscription deepened the gulf between French and English Canadians.

On the other hand, Canada's soldiers won for themselves and their country much glory by the way they fought against great odds, at battles like Ypres and Vimy Ridge. We have seen that Prime Minister Robert Borden was able to parlay Canada's sacrifices during the war to win greater recognition for Canada on the world stage, and more **autonomy** from Great Britain. As well, women finally won the vote, to a large extent because of their contributions to the war effort.

Optimism was the key again to the national mood during the 1920s, but again this was shattered by the hardships of the Great Depression and then by Canada's involvement in World War II. The United Nations was founded in 1945, the same year World War II ended, with the primary goal of ensuring that another world war would never happen.

From the very beginning, Canada was at the forefront of the UN's efforts to secure world peace. A Canadian, Lester Pearson, first suggested and then helped design the UN's peacekeeping force. For this he won the Nobel Peace Prize. Canada is the only country in the world that has participated in every one of the UN's peacekeeping efforts since they began in 1956.

Three times during the 1990s the UN has named Canada the best country in the world in which to live, beating out such prosperous rivals as the United States, Japan, and Germany. Perhaps Wilfrid Laurier's prediction has come true. What do you think? Has Canada earned the right to call the 20th century its own?

The Future

If, at the end of the 20th century, we put ourselves in Wilfrid Laurier's shoes and try to make a prediction about the next century, what can we say? Shall we be optimists or pessimists? On what signs or trends should we base our predictions?

Canada's commitment to international organizations like the Commonwealth and La Francophonie remains strong. Support for the UN is reflected in Canada's financial contributions to it. Canada is one of 78 countries out of a total of 185 that fully pays its annual dues to the UN. This compares favourably with the U.S., which owes approximately $1.3 billion in back dues.

Figure 42-1   This photo from 1987 shows three Canadian World War I veterans by the monument to Canadian soldiers atop Vimy Ridge. The ceremony marked the 70th anniversary of the battle in which more than 3500 Canadians were killed. What effect did this battle have on the national consciousness?

THE 10 BEST PLACES TO LIVE IN THE WORLD

1.	Canada	(0.950)
2.	United States	(0.938)
3.	Japan	(0.937)
4.	Netherlands	(0.936)
5.	Finland	(0.934)
6.	Iceland	(0.933)
7.	Norway	(0.933)
8.	France	(0.931)
9.	Spain	(0.930)
10.	Sweden	(0.929)

Source: Report on Business Magazine, *"The Best and Worst Places,"* 1996, pp. 18-19.

Figure 42-2 The United Nation's Human Development Index identifies Canada as the best place in the world in which to live. This index measures the quality of life in a country by considering not just average income, but also factors such as political freedom, the environment, and racial and gender equality.

Figure 42-3 In his 1962 book *The Gutenberg Galaxy*, the Canadian thinker Marshall McLuhan said: "The new electronic interdependence recreates the world in the image of a global village." What do you think McLuhan meant by this observation?

Canada regards membership in NATO as essential to its security. Recently some of the former Warsaw pact countries, including Poland, Hungary, and the Czech Republic, have been accepted into NATO, strengthening the organization and putting an end to the old Cold War rivalries. Still, threats could come from other places in the world.

Canada has also recognized that its growth and security in the future will depend on its economic relations with the rest of the world. Today, countries can no longer make decisions as if they lived in isolation and had total control over their own economies. Most of the countries in the developed world are now part of one or another large trading blocks. This is why Canada belongs to the **North American Free Trade Association (NAFTA)**.

Canadians tend to be too modest about their accomplishments and overlook the things they do well. It was a Canadian thinker, Marshall McLuhan, who coined the term **global village**. He predicted that advances in communications technology would make the countries of the world more dependent on each other for their common prosperity.

Canadians have invented many useful and entertaining things, from basketball to Pablum to computer-ordered pizzas. When we look at the flights of the space shuttles in the NASA program, we always see the Canadarm putting satellites into space. Several Canadians have also flown on these exciting missions. Roberta Bondar, Mark Garneau, Chris Hadfield, Steven Maclean, and Robert Thirsk are Canadian astronauts who are adding to the next century's scientific knowledge.

This ability to innovate is one of Canada's most valuable resources. In the end, that is where the hope for the country's future lies—in the Canadian people. You yourself have the chance to help decide what Canada's future will be, not by what you say but by what you do in the 21st century.

RECONNECT

1. Look back through this book and make a list of some of the successes and failures Canada has experienced in the 20th century. For each entry in your list tell how it could help us prepare for life in the 21st century.

2. Ideally, what kind of country would you like Canada to be in the year 2025?

GLOSSARY

ace a fighter pilot who has shot down at least five enemy aircraft.

alliance an agreement between two or more countries, usually formalized by a treaty, to protect one another in case of attack.

amphibious capable of living on land or water; in military terms, an operation involving troops attacking from the sea.

apartheid segregation based on race.

autonomy a nation's right to independence or self-government.

Balkans the countries in southeastern Europe that are surrounded by the Aegean, Adriatic and Black Sea.

blighty a wound serious enough to send a World War I soldier to hospital but not bad enough to cause lasting damage.

Boer a South African descended from Dutch settlers.

Canadian Patriotic Front a nation-wide charity founded during World War I to support soldiers' families. A private in the Canadian Armed Forces was paid $1.10 a day, a wage that was never raised during the course of the war.

canteen a shop on a military base that sells food and drink.

capitalism an economic system based on private investment and profit-making.

clan a group of people with a common ancestor.

communism an economic system based on public ownership of all property and on workers being paid according to their needs and abilities.

conscription compulsory military service.

court martial a court used to try people in the armed forces.

creeping barrage an artillery barrage that moves just ahead of attacking troops.

critical mass the minimum amount of material needed to begin or maintain a nuclear chain reaction.

cushy same as blighty (see definition above).

dogfight close combat between two or more aircraft.

enemy alien a person living in a country that is at war with his or her native country. In Canada, people have been declared enemy aliens even after they were granted status as Canadian citizens.

entrepreneur a person who organizes a business that may either succeed or fail.

epicentre in reference to a bomb, the exact point at which the bomb explodes.

espionage the practice of spying.

Fascist a member of an extreme right-wing political party in Italy from 1922 to 1943.

Fourteen Points U.S. President Woodrow Wilson's plan to ensure world peace after World War I. The Fourteen Points outlined generous terms for Germany's surrender, political freedom for all the peoples of Europe, disarmament, free trade, and freedom of the seas. The fourteenth point recommended establishing the League of Nations.

franchise the right to vote.

Fritz a derogatory name for a German soldier.

Front the scene of actual fighting between two armies.

Geneva Conventions a series of international agreements drawn up at Geneva, Switzerland between 1846 and 1949 with the aim of lessening the harm done to civilian populations during war. They also set out regulations for hospitals, ambulances, and the care of the wounded and prisoners of war.

glasnost the Russian word for "openness." Glasnost became an official policy of Mikhail Gorbachev's government.

global village the whole world considered as a single village that is linked together by telecommunications devices.

guerrilla warfare attacks carried out by small bands of soldiers fighting independently.

Hawker Hurricane one of the two most common British fighter planes during World War II, playing a major role in the Battle of Britain. The other was the Spitfire.

Holocaust the mass-murder of European Jews by the Nazis from 1941 to 1945.

Kaiser the leader of Germany at the time of World War I and earlier. The word comes from the Latin word *Caesar*.

Lend-Lease a 1941 agreement between the U.S. and Great Britain. The U.S. loaned Britain equipment and supplies in return for the use of some British military bases.

Manhattan Project code name for the American project begun in 1942 to develop the first atomic bomb.

middle power a nation without the military might or wealth to make it a superpower, but with enough resources and the political stability to give it some influence in world affairs.

nationalize to take over something (private property or property belonging to another country) on behalf of the state in which the property lies.

neutrality the condition of not supporting either of two opposing parties, especially nations at war with each other.

Nisei in Canada and the U.S., a Japanese whose parents were immigrants from Japan.

North America Free Trade Association (NAFTA) A treaty concluded among Canada, the U.S., and Mexico in 1994 that eliminated most tariffs and encouraged investment among the three countries.

parapet a wall of dirt or stone erected to protect troops from enemy fire.

perestroika the Russian word for "restructuring." It was the word used to refer to Mikhail Gorbachev's reform program in the 1980s.

posthumously after death.

propaganda the art of controlling public opinion.

puttee a long strip of cloth wound around the leg for protection from the ankle to the knee.

reconnaissance a military survey of a region, especially for locating the enemy's position.

repatriation restoring someone to his or her native land.

RAF the Royal Air Force, the airborne arm of the British armed forces.

saturation bombing heavy aerial bombardment.

scapegoat a person who bears the blame for the ills or shortcomings of others.

shell shock a nervous breakdown resulting from exposure to battle.

Soviet Bloc the collection of countries allied to or controlled by the Soviet Union from 1945 to 1991.

SS an abbreviation of the German word *Schutz-Staffel*, a special police force under Hitler.

stereotype a preconceived or unjustified notion of how a certain group of people will behave.

suffrage the right to vote in an election.

tactics the science of ordering and organizing troops during the course of a battle.

terrorism the use of violence and intimidation to achieve political goals.

Tommy a slang term for the British foot soldier.

trench foot a painful foot condition caused by long submersion in water or mud and marked by the blackening and death of the surface tissue.

trench mouth inflammation of the gums.

ultimatum a threat or a final warning that something will happen unless specific conditions are met.

veto the right of a member of the UN Security Council to reject a resolution. Veto come from the Latin word for "I forbid."

Victoria Cross the highest military decoration in the British Commonwealth. It was founded by Queen Victoria in 1856. The medals are made from guns captured by the British army at Sevastopol during the Crimean War.

Victory Bond bonds first issued by the Canadian government during World War I. The money collected was used to finance the war effort.

Victory Stamp stamps that were issued to help finance government expenditures during World War I.

war profiteer a person who seeks excessively high profits by supplying necessary items during times of war.

wolf pack an attacking group of submarines.